The Year My Mother Came Back

THE YEAR
MY MOTHER
CAME BACK

Alice Eve Cohen

ALGONQUIN BOOKS OF CHAPEL HILL 2015

Published by
ALGONQUIN BOOKS OF CHAPEL HILL
Post Office Box 2225
Chapel Hill, North Carolina 27515-2225

a division of
WORKMAN PUBLISHING
225 Varick Street
New York, New York 10014

Published simultaneously in Canada by Thomas Allen & Son Limited.
Design by Anne Winslow.

Library of Congress Cataloging-in-Publication Data
Cohen, Alice Eve.
The year my mother came back : a memoir/
by Alice Eve Cohen.—First Edition.
pages cm
ISBN 978-1-61620-319-1 (HC)
1. Cohen, Alice Eve. 2. Mothers and daughters—United States—
Biography. 3. Motherhood—United States—Biography. 4. Parent and
child—United States—Biography. 5. Children with disabilities—United
States—Biography. 6. Cohen, Alice Eve—Family. 7. Jewish
women—United States—Biography. I. Title.
HQ755.85.C6193 2015
306.874'3092—dc23
[B]   2014031973

10 9 8 7 6 5 4 3 2 1
First Edition

For
my mother
and
my daughters

Author's Note

As this is a memoir, my telling of the events in this book is filtered through the lens of memory and emotion and has been altered by the passage of time. I've changed names and identifying details of some individuals to protect their privacy. Conversations and dialogues have been modified by memory and sometimes intentionally compressed and reshaped for narrative purposes. I have also included the dreams and fantasies that were an integral part of my experience, which took place only in my imagination and on these pages.

The Year My Mother Came Back

PART 1

"What we, or at any rate what I, refer to confidently as a memory—meaning a moment, a scene, a fact that has been subjected to a fixative and thereby rescued from oblivion—is really a form of storytelling that goes on continually in the mind and often changes with the telling."

—WILLIAM MAXWELL,
So Long, See You Tomorrow

One day, my brilliant, beautiful, complicated mother appeared at my kitchen table, thirty-one years after her death.

This is a story of mothers and daughters. My mother, my daughters. My mother's daughters, my daughters' mothers. This is the story of a year.

ONE

She pulled the blue-checkered dish towel off the mixing bowl. The dough was twice as big as it was an hour ago. My mother was amused by my open-mouthed astonishment. Her smile was beautiful, colored with bright red lipstick.

"Punch it down, Honeylamb."

The dough was warm and elastic, deflating under my tiny fists, exhaling a sweet, earthy smell. When it was back to its original size, she emptied it onto the floured board, and it surrendered to her confident hands.

"Your turn, Alice."

I jabbed. I poked.

"Like this." She stood behind me, reached around my shoulders, and placed her hands on the dough. I put my hands on hers. She pushed forward with the heel of her palm, folded it back, forward, back, we kneaded in unison, like rowing a boat, like our purring cat scratching the sofa, like Daddy waltzing me around while I stood on his feet, like Mommy giving me a backrub at bedtime. I basked in the euphoria of her touch.

I wipe my tear-streaked face with the back of my hand, surprised and embarrassed to be crying in the schoolyard on a hot Friday afternoon, waiting to pick up Eliana. One more week of school. A sparrow takes two staccato hops toward me on the green wooden bench. A gust of wind blows my long hair in all directions. The sparrow flies away.

Why am I crying? Why am I thinking about my mother so much today?

Oh, yeah. Because it's June.

I don't think about Mom anymore. Well, not much. Once in a long while, in fits and starts. I sometimes find myself writing about her, my fingers typing her onto the page, unbidden. On the Jewish High Holidays, the two days in the year I go to synagogue, I think about her while reciting the Mourner's Kaddish, the prayer for the dead, which I read phonetically, having never learned Hebrew. Sometimes I dream about her, but I rarely remember the details.

And every year in late June, I suddenly get sad and wonder why I'm crying, until I remember that Mom died in June. Thirty-one years ago. June 29, 1977. My summer-solstice mood swing takes me by surprise every year, even though it's as predictable as the days getting warmer. By the start of July, it's over.

Thirty-one years is a long time. My mother has become a character from a story I used to know; a face from an old photograph, the colors faded, her features blurry. Sensory fragments emerge—the smell of her hair, the warmth of her hands, the melody of her voice, the sound of her typing and typing and typing.

I used to think about Mom all the time, the good parts and the bad parts. After she died, my thoughts would reflexively turn to her. I'd have an impulse to pick up the phone and call her, catch up on the day's events, tell her when I'd fallen in love, invite her to my performances. In darker moods, I'd want to summon her to our old battlegrounds, to demand explanation and apology, or offer my own.

Over time, I stopped wishing for her. With great effort, I stopped thinking about her. It hurt too much, too closely resembled the angst of unrequited love. Now I can't remember what I tried so hard to forget. I exiled her, like banishing an errant ex-boyfriend from my thoughts; burying my memories of her as deep as I could, so my unrelieved longing for her—and my anger at her—would go away.

Except in June.

Every June she's in my thoughts, whether I want her there or not.

I picture my mother the last time I saw her, when she told me, "This is the first time in years that I am truly happy."

The school bell rings. I look for Eliana's third-grade class in the sea of children streaming out the doors into the sunbaked schoolyard, giddy in anticipation of summer vacation.

TWO

Eliana approaches the finish line, her long braids swinging from side to side as she runs. She looks unmistakably like Michael's daughter—same light brown, wavy hair, fair complexion, and slightly crooked grin. No trace of my Mediterranean looks, dark straight hair, dark eyes, olive complexion. Eliana's luminous green eyes, which change color depending on the light, are hers alone.

Her gait at the end of three miles is slightly off-kilter, a dancerly step-leap, step-leap, step-leap. She puts less weight on her right foot, which is not as cushioned, because of the inflexible shoe lift. Her right leg is three inches shorter than the left. Her head tilts slightly to the right, compensating for the shorter side of her body, something she does when she's tired or when her muscles are tight, a distant echo of her infant scoliosis. When she was born, her tiny, asymmetrical body was curved like the letter C. The doctor said she might never walk. Today, she ran three miles!

She runs under the arch of purple balloons and joins her team, ten ebullient girls jumping up and down in a group hug. Today is the culminating event of the citywide after-school program, Girls on the Run. We head over to celebrate with a team breakfast on the pier, which the city has recently transformed from an abandoned wreck of rotting wood into an idyllic park with a sublime view of the Statue of Liberty.

This was an extraordinary year for Eliana. When she was younger, she couldn't keep up with other kids. Now, she's one of the fastest girls at tag. It took Eliana's determination and the joint efforts (pun intended) of her gifted physical therapists, from the time she was two months old, to straighten her curved spine, overcome the physical challenges of asymmetry, and—like personal trainers coaching a diminutive Olympian—maximize her athletic potential.

For the first time in her life, she's as tall as other kids her age. Since kindergarten, she has taken a daily injection of growth hormone to compensate for her growth disorder. Even more impressive than these physical gains, with the attentive guidance of her third-grade teacher, she's evolved from an insecure and shy seven-year-old into a socially and academically confident eight-year-old. At the beginning of third grade she hated writing and said she was terrible at it. Last week, she wrote:

Poem about Poem
1 cup of starting and a half a cup done,
3 cups of creativity, and 2 cups of fun,
3 cups of friendly, and 2 cups of mean,
2 tablespoons of king, and a half a cup of queen,
3 cups of faraway, and 2 cups of home,
and all that's a recipe, for one tiny poem!

The girls sprint ahead of their parents, making a beeline for the sprinkler. Michael takes my hand, and I get that same adrenaline rush I felt when I fell in love with him twelve years ago.

This past year has been a period of relative calm in our marriage, now that our worry about Eliana has subsided. At our wedding, Eliana was six months old and Julia was nine: we jumped directly from fiancés to stressed-out married couple with kids. Ten years younger than me, Michael was like a kid himself when we met, but he grew up fast in order to keep our family in one piece, giving up freelancing for a more stable career in corporate communications. His bio now reads, "Michael used to create comic performances for corporate audiences, where he portrayed, parodied, and spoofed business executives—before becoming one himself."

For me, this past year was about seeking absolution from my most unforgiving judge: me. I'm making slow progress toward assuaging my maternal guilt. The onset of that guilt was nine years ago. Michael and I had just gotten engaged, when I started to feel sick. My doctor said it was menopause, but I kept feeling worse. After months of doctors' visits and tests, I was raced to an emergency CAT scan for an abdominal tumor, which turned out not to be a tumor at all. I was six months pregnant.

I desperately didn't want to have a baby. There was evidence that the fetus had been injured—by X rays, CAT scans, and my daily dose of prescription hormones, known to cause birth defects. I was in shock—it was fourteen years after I'd received a diagnosis of infertility, with no chance of ever becoming pregnant; it was nine years after adopting Julia. I felt trapped and *terrified*. My suicidal thoughts made late-term abortion a legal option, and I scheduled an appointment in Wichita, Kansas, one of only three clinics nationwide that provided abortions in the third trimester. I had exactly one week to make an impossible decision. At the eleventh hour, I chose to have the baby.

After giving birth to Eliana, I plummeted into the purgatory of postpartum depression. I was sure her shorter leg and other medical problems were my fault. I was guilty of prenatal neglect: unintentional, but in my depression-addled mind, unforgivable. I was so confused and full of remorse—for wanting to abort, and for injuring her in utero—that I kept all of it a secret.

I've recently begun to share the story of my terrifying pregnancy. My friends don't judge or despise me for it, as I'd feared. But one day (a day I dread), I will have to tell Eliana the harrowing story of her birth—a conversation I hope to postpone for as long as possible.

THE GIRLS DASH from the sprinkler to their mothers' laps, soaking wet, teeth chattering, exhausted from the run. We wrap our daughters in colorful beach towels and hand them water bottles. They sleepily drink from their bottles, lying in the sun, curled up in our laps, like when they were babies. The wind picks up. Eliana is shivering. I wrap my arms and the yellow towel around her more tightly, and her wet body begins to warm.

The wind picked up, whipping my long hair around my face. Mom led us across the seaweed-strewn wet sand at low tide. Madeline was twelve, Jennifer was five, and I was eight. My sisters and I were dressed in matching blue one-piece bathing suits. Mom was wearing her yellow-striped sundress. The foamy waves rolled over our feet, tangling our ankles in long strands of seaweed, and sculpting ephemeral footprints, which disappeared with each new wave.

"'Private Property, No Trespassing,'" Madeline read aloud.

"Ignore the sign!" said Mom.

"Won't we get arrested?" I asked, with equal parts trepidation and excitement.

"No. We're below the high-tide mark, so we're not breaking the law. The point is, girls, that all beachfront should be public access. That's what we're fighting for. It's unforgivable that rich people are the only ones who get to enjoy this glorious coastline. That's why we're protesting. Do you understand?"

I nodded. Madeline shrugged her shoulders. Jennifer chased a fiddler crab.

We kept walking across the low-tide wet sand, tossing stones into the surf, chasing seagulls and terns, skirting barnacle-encrusted rocks, till we got to a secluded area marked by a wooden fence and another sign:

PRIVATE BEACH. KEEP OUT.
TRESPASSERS WILL BE PROSECUTED.
CHILMARK POLICE DEPARTMENT
MARTHA'S VINEYARD, MASSACHUSSETS.

A palatial beach-house sat above the dune, the sea and sky reflected in enormous picture windows. A weathered, wooden stairway, overgrown with sea grass and beach plum, led from the beach over the dune and up to the sundeck, where two women in bikinis and a man in plaid shorts were having drinks. The man stood and waved his arms, shooing us away.

"This is where we stop, girls. Right here." She ignored the man and sat down on the wet sand, facing the ocean.

"Not cool," said Madeline under her breath. The four of us sat side by side on the sloping shore.

"Isn't it beautiful here?" said Mom.

"I'm cold," said Jennifer.

"HELLO! EXCUSE ME," shouted the man on the sun deck, competing with the sound of the wind and surf. "THIS IS A PRIVATE BEACH!"

Mommy turned to face him, and shouted back through the wind, "NO, SIR, YOU ARE MISTAKEN."

"WHAT DID YOU SAY?"

"I SAID, WE'RE BELOW THE HIGH-TIDE LINE, SO THIS IS NOBODY'S PROPERTY."

Mom was brave, the way she stood up to him, and really smart.

The man threw his hands up in exasperation and went into the house. The ladies in bikinis continued to sip their drinks, smirking.

"You sure we won't get arrested?" I asked.

"Absolutely not! We haven't broken the law."

"I'm cold," Jennifer said again, shivering in the salty spray.

"Then run around. But don't swim, because there's no lifeguard. And watch out for sharks."

"Aw, I wish I could go swimming," said Jennifer.

"Sharks need more than three inches of water, Mom," said Madeline.

"You can't be too careful when it comes to sharks."

Jennifer collected shells and seaweed. Madeline waded in the waves. I sat next to Mom. It was exciting when she fought for things like this. I loved when she took us on adventures. I mean protests. You never knew how it would turn out. It made me feel important to sit on the sand beside her. We were fighting for something together.

After a while, a tall, thin policeman walked down the beach toward us. He looked out of place in his uniform. The man in plaid shorts came back out onto his deck with his arms folded over his chest, watching us.

"Oh, no," groaned Madeline. She and Jennifer watched from a safe distance, while I inched closer to Mom on the wet sand. I was a little scared of the policeman, in case he arrested us.

"Good afternoon, Ma'am," said the policeman.

"Good afternoon, Officer. Isn't it a gorgeous day?"

"Ya see that sign?"

"Yes, Officer, we read the sign."

"Do you know what trespassing means?"

"Of course. But we're not trespassing."

The policeman was confused. "This is a private beach. Belongs to that man up there." He pointed to that man up there.

"No, it doesn't. We're below the high-tide line, so this isn't private property, his or anybody else's."

"Lady! The high-tide ordinance is for boat-owners.

You're allowed to bring your boat up close to a private beach, for fishing or whatever, as long as you're below the high-tide line."

"Alas, we forgot to bring our boat with us today. But whatever the intent of the law, my daughters and I are within our legal rights, and we intend to stay here until the tide is high, which is hours from now." She smiled at him, friendly as can be, and a little bit flirty.

The policeman glanced at Mom's cleavage. He looked up at the man on the sundeck and shrugged his shoulders, then wagged his finger at my mom. "You better not cross the line," he said, pointing behind us at the uninterrupted ribbon of blackened seaweed, pale driftwood, shell shards, desiccated jellyfish, and other flotsam and jetsam separating the wet sand from the dry beach.

"I'll be back." He turned and sauntered back down the beach.

"Do we really have to stay here till high tide?" I asked, when the policeman was out of earshot.

"No. We just had to make a point," said Mom. "Come here, girls. Now listen, if you never question the rules, nothing will ever change. That police officer will never think about waterfront access the same way."

"Yeah, never," I agreed.

"Maybe," said Madeline.

We played by the shore a while longer, chasing sand-pipers and scuttling hermit crabs, till the tide began to rise.

"I'm freezing," said Jennifer, jumping from foot to foot.

"Me, too." I was beginning to shiver.

"Let's go, girls. Good work."

"That was fun," I said.

We retraced our steps, jumping over clamshells, stranded jellyfish, and foamy surf, back to the crowded public beach.

Jennifer's teeth were chattering. Mom wrapped her in a big, yellow towel and cuddled her in her lap.

The Girls on the Run picnic is winding down. Eliana snuggles drowsily in my lap. In one week, she finishes third grade, and Julia graduates from high school. Last Saturday was Julia's senior prom. In two months, she leaves for college. (College! How did that happen?)

I stroke my younger daughter's wet hair. Eliana ran three miles today.

It's a day of pure happiness.

So of course, I'm counting the days till Doomsday.

Doomsday is scheduled for August 6.

THE GOOD NEWS: Eliana is going to have surgery to lengthen her shorter leg.

The bad news: Eliana is going to have surgery to lengthen her shorter leg.

"She'll need two surgeries: a first to lengthen her upper leg; a second one to lengthen her lower leg," said Dr. Campbell in January, after reviewing Eliana's X rays and growth curve, and describing the long, arduous limb-lengthening procedure to us in grueling detail.

"Is it absolutely necessary?" I asked.

(All surgery terrifies me. My idea of preventive surgery is to prevent surgery.)

"The question is not *whether* she'll have surgery; it's *when*. Without surgery, she'll have back pain her entire life. This is a good age for her to have her first leg-lengthening. She should complete the second one by high school."

"Does it hurt?" Eliana asked him.

"Yes, but we'll give you medicine to take care of the pain."

"When will I be a hundred percent better?"

"It takes eight months."

"I just want to get it over with. As long as I can go to camp. That's the most important thing to me."

"Okay, here's what I propose," he said, sitting beside Eliana on the examining table. "Go to camp this summer. We'll do the surgery when you get back in August. That way, you'll be fully recovered by April, and you can go to camp again next summer. Do we have a deal?"

Dr. Campbell extended his hand.

Eliana shrugged and shook his hand.

I took Eliana to two more surgeons for second and third opinions, hoping they would tell me that she didn't need surgery at all, that she was doing just fine with a shoe lift. Heck, she plays on the West Side Soccer League; she can run three miles. I was looking for a surgeon who shared my "If it ain't broke, don't fix it" credo. But all three surgeons had the same opinion—not the one I was looking for. I wish I could kiss Eliana's boo-boo and make it better, the way my mom took care of my garden-variety scrapes and bruises. But Eliana's growth disorder is an über boo-boo, requiring Herculean measures.

Eliana's surgery is scheduled for August 6 with Dr. Campbell. I dread it, but like Eliana, I just want to get it over with. I am determined to be the unwavering, un-ambivalent, dedicated mother Eliana will need me to be, for the duration of her eight-month medical ordeal.

THREE

....

I stare blankly at my computer on the kitchen table, where I've been writing all afternoon, and try unsuccessfully to see this as an *Aha!* moment instead of an *Oh, shit!* moment. My doctor called me three minutes ago, on this steamy July afternoon, with the news that I have breast cancer.

I call Michael at work, but he doesn't pick up. "Please call when you get this," I say, with just enough urgency to motivate him to call me back.

I put my face in my hands and cry for a few minutes, lonely and scared.

I call my sisters at their offices, but Madeline and Jennifer aren't picking up their phones. Julia is in Canada all month. Eliana is at camp in Maine till Thursday.

This doesn't fit into my plans to be a perfect mother, completely available to Eliana. I was so preoccupied with her surgery, scheduled eleven days from now, that I forgot to look over my shoulder, and the Evil Eye snuck up behind me.

Michael wouldn't believe me if I confessed to him that I literally feared the Evil Eye. He assumes I use it as a literary device, which is only partially true. I haven't told Michael the part where I believe the Evil Eye is breathing down my neck, waiting for my next misstep. I've tried to overcome my fear of unguarded happiness (the green light for the Evil Eye), but my fear is tenacious.

My slip-up might have been three months ago, in April, when I joyfully e-mailed my friends from college to share the good news that Julia got into Princeton, our alma mater. Joanne e-mailed back, *"i'm so happy for julia, (and for you!) my advice is, if you haven't yet, turn a glass over. if you don't know about turning a glass over, my grandma used to swear by it. it kept the bad spirits away when something good happened."*

I thought I already knew all the necessary precautions for keeping away bad spirits. I learned them from my mother, decades ago: "Always throw spilled salt over your left shoulder." Done. "Spit three times between the middle and index fingers to keep away the Evil Eye," *Tuh, tuh, tuh!*—Done. (I ignored her more phobic precautions, which caused her to cower in the middle of a room during an electrical storm and prevented her from taking elevators—she climbed many flights of stairs, long before it was promoted for exercise.) "Don't gloat over good news, and above all," she taught me by example, "don't admit that you're truly happy." Oops, forgot that one.

Joanne's grandma's upside-down glass ritual was new to me, but there was logic to it; the upturned glass would keep the bad spirits out, like keeping a genie in a bottle, or the lid closed on Pandora's box. I promptly turned over the empty glass on my desk and e-mailed Joanne with a pragmatic follow-up question: "How long did your grandma say you should keep the glass upside-down?"

No response. Maybe Joanne thought I was kidding. Maybe *she* was kidding. Maybe she never read my e-mail. The next night, I put the upside-down glass in the dishwasher. The Evil Eye must have escaped before the rinse cycle.

The cancer showed up on a routine mammogram. During the biopsy, a small metal marker was inserted, to make it easier to find the tumor at a later date. Unfortunately, the metal marker is now sitting on a nerve. For the past week, at random moments while walking down the street, a sudden shooting pain has caused me to involuntarily utter a loud yelp and grab my left breast with my right hand—*"YELP!" Grab*—which must look bizarre to passersby, who probably think I have a unique version of Tourette syndrome—*"YELP!" Grab*—Excruciating in the moment, but not a lingering pain. Embarrassing, but—*"YELP!" Grab*—out of my control. The silver lining of my doctor's call this morning was her promise that the metal marker would be removed, along with the lump.

I'm not surprised by the diagnosis. My mother had breast cancer when she was forty-seven. I was twelve, on the cusp of puberty, the summer after seventh grade. Mom survived cancer, but she died of a stroke ten years later, when she was fifty-seven, five years older than I am now.

I close my eyes. I hear a familiar percussive sound. I open my eyes.

My mother is at the kitchen table next to me, typing on her old-fashioned black manual typewriter, fingers flying over the keys.

What is she doing here? My mother has been dead for thirty-one years.

I think about her every June, but this is the middle of

July. I don't think about her in July. Yet here she is, typing furiously. Here, in my head, in my apartment, sitting beside me at the kitchen table. My brilliant, beautiful, complicated mother.

"What are you doing here?"

"Typing," she says, barely looking up from her work.

"But you're dead." She stops now, looks up at me.

"I know."

A salty breeze blows through my kitchen and wraps itself around me. It is my mother's hug from fifty years ago, when I was a very little girl. It makes me cry.

"Mommy, I'm sick."

"That's why I'm here."

I see her more vividly than I have in the three decades since she died. Her fingers race over the clacking keys of the Smith Corona, the same typewriter she's had since she was a Barnard student in the 1940s. She stares intently at the keyboard, warm brown eyes magnified by thick glasses; her face, once chiseled and gorgeous, now softly wrinkled, framed by cropped gray curls. She wears a yellow button-down shirt and blue wraparound skirt. Life-sized and adamantly unconventional—legs unshaven, hair undyed, chest flat and un-enhanced, warmblooded, 3-D Technicolor. Mom is sitting right next to me, extracted from the cosmic periphery to which I've relegated her for thirty-one years.

"I have breast cancer."

"I know. So did I. I know all about breast cancer."

YEAH, SHE KNEW about it. Mom had a double radical mastectomy, all her lymph nodes removed, and some of the flesh and muscle from both armpits. In 1967, lumpectomy was not an option. Breast surgery was an all or nothing deal. My mother had it all, and ended up with nothing.

On the last day of seventh grade, Dad helped Mom into the car and drove her to the hospital, without telling us why. Days passed. I was scared she would die. Two weeks passed. I was sure she was dead. When she came back home from the hospital, she looked and acted like a different person. So sad and thin, flat-chested, suddenly gray-haired, weak and old.

My mom didn't actually die, but she was gone.

Now she's in my kitchen, typing.

My mother was writing her PhD dissertation the summer she was diagnosed with cancer. She was always working on her dissertation, which she never finished. From the time I was able to grasp a crayon in my toddler fist, the backs of her discarded pages were my drawing paper. I sat beside her with my Crayola box, drawing and drawing and drawing.

For the first time in decades, I'm remembering Mom, all of her—the wonderful and terrible things about her that I've cast out of my thoughts for so long. I'm still struggling to prevent these memories from erupting from their subterranean depths. Trying to hold back the flood. I can't, not today. The levees break.

My breast cancer has brought my mother back to me.

But now is not the time. My daughters need me, Eliana most of all. I have to be unwavering in my maternal commitment. I'm trying to be a great mother, but my experience as a daughter is still haunting me. I don't want my mother here. Not now. I don't want to think about her, or how our once-close relationship devolved into barbed mistrust. She's a liability. She'll get in the way.

But she's back.

She stops typing, pushes her reading glasses on top of her head, rests her elbows on the table with fingers laced together, and looks at me expectantly. What does she want?

It seems perversely ordinary to have my mother sitting

here with me in my kitchen. I should make us a pot of coffee, but she's a ghost. I guess. Is that what she is? I don't know what to call this version of her. I'm scared of ghosts, they remind me of death. What if my mother's ghost has come for me, like the Grim Reaper? I'm nearly the same age she was when she died. Maybe she wants to take me with her. But I don't believe in ghosts, so this is not possible, which means my mother sitting here at the kitchen table with me is really, really bad.

I close my eyes.

Send her away. Bury her. Forget her, like I have—very effectively, thank you very much—for the past thirty years. I don't have time for my mother's ghost, or for this uncompromising torrent of memories, or my holographic fantasy of her, or whoever and whatever she is. It's not safe. It's not practical. There's so much to figure out. I don't have time for her right now!

Open my eyes.

She's still there. Shit.

Close my eyes. Inhale.

Yit-ga-dal ve-yit-ka-dash—I stumble through the few Hebrew syllables I remember from the Mourner's Kaddish—*she-mei ra-ba* . . . I don't know what it means, but

I hope it encourages her to go back to wherever she came from.

Go away! Go!

Open my eyes.

She's gone. Thank God! Exhale.

FOUR

The summer suddenly has a different temporal landscape. Eliana comes home from camp in two days. She assumes that she's having surgery on August 6, a week after she gets back. Her surgery will be the start of a grueling eight-month process of painful leg-lengthening.

But now *I'm* scheduled for surgery at the end of August, followed by six weeks of radiation. I'm very lucky: my cancer is zero grade, noninvasive, garden-variety DCIS, *ductal carcinoma in situ,* the most common type of breast cancer. It's completely curable. *(Tuh, tuh, tuh!)* Even so, Eliana's surgeon and mine concur: leg-lengthening can wait; cancer cannot. Eliana's surgery will be postponed until after my radiation treatment is finished.

BEFORE CALLING ELIANA at camp, I rehearse what I'm going to say, so I won't cry. But as soon as I hear her voice—light, airy, high-pitched, full of little girl excitement and wonder and love and trust—I am choking back tears. I love her so much. I tell her, using as few words as possible, so that I can get out a complete thought without falling apart, that her surgery will be postponed until November.

"Why?"

"Because . . ." I speak slowly and carefully, to maintain my composure. "I need to have surgery in August, and my doctor says we can't both have surgery at the same time."

"Aw. I wanted to get it over with. Now I have to worry about surgery all the way to November."

"I know. I'm sorry."

"Will I still be completely better by April?"

"No."

"Aw. That's not fair."

"I know."

"Will I be better in time for camp next year?"

"Yes. And the good news is, you're free for the rest of this summer. If you want to, you can stay at camp an extra two weeks. What do you think?"

Brief pause.

"I want to come home. I love camp, but I'm homesick,

too, in a good way. I've already packed. I want to come home tomorrow."

And then I love her and miss her so much, I'm crying again. I can't wait to see her. I'm so happy she wants to come home, so happy I'll see her tomorrow, and that we'll be together for the rest of the summer. So glad she didn't take me up on my offer.

The next day, Eliana's bus from camp is delayed. I have an hour to kill, so I stroll to Lincoln Center and sit on the edge of the fountain. The plumes of water, the hot afternoon sun, the cool mist, and the roar of water are hypnotic. I remember being Eliana's age, the thrall of summer vacation with my family.

Dad taught me and my sisters to bodysurf. Sand was everywhere—in my bathing suit, in my butt crack, between my toes. He was the fun one. I mean, I loved Mom, too. I loved her so much, and she was the one who brought us on protests, and who took care of us every day when Dad was at work, and if we were ever sick. But he was more fun, he played more, he liked games.

Our sunburns were tanned from long, sunny, salty days on the beach. The summer was almost over.

As soon we got back home from vacation, Dad sat down at the piano. While he played Beethoven, Mom announced, "I'm going outside to read." That was her way of saying she was going to take a nap, without admitting it. In five minutes, she was asleep in the hammock with a book on her chest. She snored softly, which Jennifer and I thought was hilarious. We watched her from the living room window and giggled. It was good to be home.

A chickadee flew onto the hammock right next to sleeping Mom. Then a robin redbreast. Birds loved my Mom. They must have missed her while we were away on vacation. I took out binoculars and my field guide to birds. Two sparrows. A tufted titmouse. A bright red cardinal. Mom had a knack of getting along with nature. She just understood. I don't know how she did it. Jennifer and I wondered why the birds wouldn't land on us, despite our efforts. We had tried lying on the hammock, as motionless as we could, but the birds never came. We dared each other to stay absolutely still for ten minutes, but we couldn't do it for even one minute. We were too jumpy. We giggled and the hammock wiggled. It was Jennifer's fault. She tickled me when I was trying not to move a muscle.

THE TALL BUTTERCUPS in our yard danced in the breeze, like they were having a party. That spring, when Dad mowed the lawn and cut down the buttercups, it broke Mom's heart, and she campaigned for buttercups' rights.

"I don't particularly like the idea," said Dad.

"Please, Ira, the wildflowers are so beautiful, and the girls love them. What if you just mow the front yard, and not the back?"

"Well, all right, Louise," he grumbled.

Since we went away for vacation three weeks before, the grass and flowers had grown higher than ever. Jennifer and I ran outside and chased each other around the back-yard. It was a meadow now, filled with buttercups, dandelions, tiger lilies, Queen Anne's lace, and goldenrod. Rose bushes in full bloom and peppermint plants with tiny purple flowers surrounded the big rock we liked to climb. Amanda, our gray cat, dove into the tall grass and proudly emerged with a mouse in her teeth.

The blue jays circled high above, cackling from a safe distance. They never landed on the hammock—the jays hated our family. They were mad at us, because this spring a newborn blue jay fell out of their nest into our yard, and I picked it up to save it. I'd been planning to put it in a shoebox and feed it mashed-up bread and milk with an eyedropper, like Mom showed me how to do with that baby sparrow I saved the previous summer. But the blue jay parents thought I was kidnapping it. Or maybe they thought I was a predator who wanted to eat their baby, so they dive-bombed my head and I had to run inside. Then I looked out the window, and saw the most horrible thing: the mother and father blue jays killed their own baby. They pecked it to death. It made me cry so much that Mommy had to hold me in her lap and comfort me. "It's okay, Alice, sweetheart. I know you were trying to save the chick, but the jays don't know that. It's in their nature to protect their domain." After that, the blue jays dive-bombed our heads every time we went out of the house. Especially my head. They were holding a grudge.

Until Mom came up with a plan.

"Alice, round up all the kids on the block and bring them over."

I ran up and down the block and got twelve kids, and we ran into my house, past the dive-bombing blue jays. Mom had assembled all our pots and spoons on the kitchen table.

"I want each of you to take a pot or a pan and a

wooden spoon. Everyone have one? Okay. Are you ready to make a lot of noise?"

"READY!" shouted twelve kids.

We went in the front yard, carrying our pots and pans. As soon as the blue jays started flying down from their tree, Mommy gave the command. "MAKE AS MUCH NOISE AS YOU CAN!"

We banged and crashed the pans and screamed our heads off. It was loud and exciting. The jays got scared and flew in circles right over our heads—we could feel the wind from their wings. They were squawking and wanted to peck us, I could tell, but they didn't. They flew in circles, higher and higher and higher.

They didn't attack us ever since then. Nor did they go near Mom.

JENNIFER AND I picked a bouquet of wildflowers and went back in the house. Dad played piano and my sisters and I danced around the living room. He sang the funny songs he learned growing up in Brooklyn. While accompanying himself on the piano, he made a pretend ugly face and sang,

There once was a man named Dirty Bill!
He lived on top of Garbage Hill.

He never took a bath and he never will.
Ach, Poo! Dirty Bill!

The three of us climbed on his lap and begged, "More, Daddy! More!" And he sang with a pretend mean face, while banging out minor chords.

Oh Dunderbeck, oh Dunderbeck, how could you be so
*   mean,*
To ever have invented the sausage meat machine?
Now all the little cats and dogs will never more be seen,
'Cause they've all been ground to sausage meat, in
*   Dunderbeck's machine.*

"More, Daddy!"
He recited a rhyme he learned when he was growing up:

"There were toidy poiple boids sitting on the coib, on da
corner of Toidy-toid and Toid, a-choipin' and a-boipin'
and a-eatin' woims. When along comes Hoib and his girl-
friend Moitle, what woiks in the shoit factory. Gee, they
was pertoibed."

He played songs from Gilbert and Sullivan, and we spun around the living room to "Three Little Girls from School Are We," from *The Mikado*.

He played "Hava Nagila." Madeline, Jennifer, and I grabbed hands and danced the hora in such a fast circle, we all got dizzy and flopped on the green couch.

Mom woke from her nap. The birds flew off the hammock, and she went into the kitchen to make dinner. I followed her and gave her the bouquet. "It's gorgeous," she said, and put in on the table in a glass jar. I helped her make a salad while the spaghetti was boiling. We set the table, nibbled on cheese and crackers and carrot sticks, and talked about birds and our vacation. I liked being in the kitchen with Mom. She was usually busy, but she always had time to talk to me while she was cooking.

After dinner, she washed the dishes in a sink full of soapsuds and I helped her dry. She put Jennifer to bed and came back to work at the kitchen table. While she typed, I sat next to her and drew a picture of our backyard, using all the colors in my crayon box.

"What a beautiful drawing, Alice."

"It's for you."

"Thank you, darling, I'll put it on the refrigerator. Time for bed."

I got in my pajamas and she tucked me in.

"Will you do 'X Marks the Spot'?"

"Sure, Sweetie."

She sat on the edge of my bed. I rolled onto my stomach, and she stroked my back with her warm hand, under my pajama top. This was my favorite thing in the whole world.

"X marks the spot, with a dot, dot, dot . . ." she recited in a soft, singing voice, her finger tracing an X and three dots, with the lightest touch.

"And a dash, and a line, and a big question mark."

Her finger drew a huge question mark on my back.

"Trickle up, trickle down. Trickle all around."

The trickling up and down and all around was the best part. It could go on indefinitely, her fingers touching my skin so softly I got goose bumps. It felt amazing. It was ecstasy. I didn't want it to stop, but it did.

"With a pinch and a squeeze, and a cool ocean breeze."

She blew gently on my back.

"Again," I murmered, almost asleep.

"X marks the spot, with a dot, dot, dot . . ."

THAT NIGHT, SOMEONE dumped garbage in our backyard. In the morning, we found the smelly heap, decomposing in the weeds. We were pretty sure the garbage was courtesy of the DiNapolis, our very mean, very fat neighbors, who ran the rooming house behind our house.

But it could have been some of our other neighbors on the block. Dad said they were angry because of our un-mowed lawn.

I climbed the tree in our yard and surveyed the neighborhood to look for clues about the garbage incident. I liked it up in the tree, where I could see everyone but no one could see me. From the tree, I heard Mrs. DiNapoli tell her husband that she was going to poison our cat if it went in their yard again. I warned Amanda to stay on our side of the fence. She was a smart cat, and she steered clear.

Three days later, when we woke up, we found our bicycles with slashed tires, and graffiti covering our driveway. Enormous black letters, painted in a child's handwriting, spelled J-E-W, big enough to reach all the way across the driveway. I had a feeling the Donahue boys at the other end of the block were responsible, because sometimes they whispered "Jew" at me and Jennifer, as if it was a bad word, when we walked past their house.

Mom and Dad had whispered conversations.

I didn't exactly know what it meant that we were Jewish, since we didn't go to synagogue or Hebrew school. I just knew we were the only Jews in the neighborhood, and now it seemed like it was the only thing about us that mattered.

Mom hired one of the teenage boys on the block to mow the lawn. "But please leave the buttercups and dandelions."

He stared at her with his mouth open for a moment. "How do you mow a lawn but leave the buttercups and dandelions?"

"Just do your best."

"Okay, Mrs. Cohen," he said, rolling his eyes. He pushed the heavy lawn mower in circles, leaving haphazard islands of tall grass and wildflowers scattered through the yard.

A week after the bicycle incident, Jennifer and I were outside eating popsicles in the front yard. The Ramirez kids, Miguel and Rosalia, were riding bikes up and down the block, and Rosalia called out, "Jennifer, Miguel loves you even though you are Jewish."

Sally from across the street came over to play. She was two years older than me, and she wasn't very nice, but not as mean as her little brother Kevin, who was my age. Kevin threw rocks at me and kicked me in the shins. But Kevin's mother and my mother were friends, and they thought we kids should play together.

Sally and I were in my room, building blocks.

"You'll never go to Heaven," Sally said, out of the blue.

"Why not?" I asked her, having no idea what Heaven was.

"Because you're Jewish."

"So what?"

"Because the Jews killed Christ."

"Why did they kill Christ?" I asked, having no idea who Christ was.

"How should I know? But that's why you can't get into Heaven."

"What's Heaven, anyway?"

"You don't know what Heaven is? You must be retarded."

"I am not retarded!" I said, having no idea what *retarded* meant.

"And your mother is crazy!"

"No, she's not."

"Yes she is. She's old and she's crazy."

"No, she's not."

"Yes, she is."

"Is not."

"Is too. Your mother is crazy."

I threw a block at Sally. It chipped her tooth, and she ran home, crying.

Eliana climbs out of the camp bus after the nine-hour ride, looking healthy and beautiful, although her long hair seems not to have been brushed for weeks. When we get home, she drops her bags in the middle of the floor and runs to her room for a reunion with Harry Potter the Hamster. Harry eagerly climbs into her hand from his cage—a large plastic globe with winding tubes and other hamster-friendly amenities. He displays his affection by sitting in her palm and exuberantly grooming himself, until he makes it clear that he's had enough socializing.

I sit Eliana down to comb her hair, gently as I can, except when the tangles require more force. She wiggles a loose tooth and tells me about her cabinmates and counselors, llamas, tie-dyeing, and marshmallow roasts. Her euphoric monologue about camp lasts all day and into the next.

"Alex is my favorite llama," she tells me while watching the sea lion feeding at the zoo. "He's a really nice guy. I took him for a walk every day."

"YELP!" Grab.

She doesn't notice my new tic. She holds my left hand, leaving me free to grab my breast with my right. "And it's true, llamas do spit when they're mad, but only at each other," she continues, while we row a boat on the Central Park Lake.

"*YELP!*" *Grab.*

"Animal care was awesome. I took care of pot-bellied pigs and rabbits and donkeys and kittens," she continues, in front of Calder's Circus at the Whitney Museum. "We fed and mucked and cleaned and brushed them. Oh, and Gross Out Day this summer was the best ever."

"*YELP!*" *Grab.*

At home, she flops down on the sofa and wiggles her tooth. "Do you have any more questions for me about camp, Mom?"

When I run out of questions, I ask, "Do you have any questions for *me*?"

"Um, yeah. Why are you having surgery?"

"Ah, good question. Because . . ."

This won't be easy. I'm determined to do this differently than my mother did. I'm not going to keep my cancer a secret from my daughters.

"Because I have breast cancer. The surgeon will remove the part with cancer. It's called a lumpectomy."

"Will you get better?"

"Yes. My doctor says I'll get completely better."

"Good."

That was easy! Was it too easy? Nah. I wish Mom had told me, when I was twelve, why she was going to the hospital. On the other hand, my doctor has assured me that my cancer is curable. Mom had no such guarantee.

"Do you have any more questions?"

"Ummm." she wiggles her tooth meditatively. "Yeah. Is there really a tooth fairy?"

"Ah . . ."

"Tell me the truth, Mom. Who puts the money under the pillow?"

I remember confronting my mother with the same question.

Sally, the mean girl across the street, had revealed the big, fat parental conspiracy. "Your mom is lying to you." "No, she's not!" "Is, too. There's no such thing as the Tooth Fairy, stupid! Only babies and retards believe in fairies!"

"You're right, Alice," my mother confessed, "I'm the one who puts the quarter under your pillow when you lose a tooth."

I burst into tears—betrayed, humiliated, and terribly sad. "Why did you lie to me?"

"It wasn't a lie, Alice. It was a fantasy. It was true for *you*. The tooth fairy is a gift parents give to their children when they're young enough to believe in fairies."

She struggled to explain a deeper truth about fairies than I was able to understand. This was my first existential crisis, and it was all the fault of mean, stupid Sally. I wasn't ready to stop believing, but there was no turning back.

However, Eliana initiated this.

"How truthful do you want me to be, Eliana?"

"Totally truthful."

"Okay. The tooth fairy isn't real. Daddy and I put the money under your pillow."

"That's what I thought."

"Any more questions?"

"Yeah. Will I still get money if I put my tooth under the pillow?"

"Yes."

"Good."

"Any more questions?"

"Um, yeah. I've been thinking about this for a while. How come I look so much more like Daddy than I look like you, when I grew up inside your body, and all Daddy did was give you a wedding ring?"

"Ah . . ."

Cancer! Tooth fairy! Sex! Whoa, isn't this a bit much for one afternoon? Eliana's questions are a checklist of the Secrets of Life. I can't wait to return to our conversations about llama care and Gross Out Day.

"I'm so glad you asked that question," I say, half-truthfully, stalling while I try to remember my parenting strategy for this moment. I do in fact have a plan, which includes visual aids. I scan the bookshelves, looking for the book I planted there a year ago.

"I bought this for you," I say, reaching to the highest shelf for a children's book about reproduction, illustrated with drawings and photographs of a ruddy-cheeked Swedish family, the father and pregnant mother uninhibitedly sharing the facts of life with their adorable little kids.

We sit on the sofa, and I begin reading. "When a man and a woman—"

"I know how to read, Mom."

"May I read it to you?"

"I'd rather read it myself." I hand her the book and watch her eyes getting wider as she reads. I hope I'm doing this right.

I was eleven years old. All the fifth-grade girls went to the auditorium to watch a movie, for girls only, about growing up. Top secret. A few of the girls giggled during the screening. I didn't get the joke. I didn't get anything. The movie made absolutely no sense to me. It was in a secret code that I couldn't decipher. There were eggs inside us girls, and once a month, our eggs might turn into babies.

Huh? Eggs? Humans? This was crazy! It couldn't be true. When we walked back to class, I started singing "I Won't Grow Up!" from *Peter Pan*, hoping the other girls would join me. I did it to get a laugh. But really and truly, I didn't want to grow up. The girls just stared at me like I was mental, so I stopped singing. I guess they actually wanted to grow up.

When we got to the classroom, the boys went to the auditorium to see the boy movie, and the girls were each given a booklet called *The Birds and the Bees: What Every Girl Should Know*, which had nothing to do with birds or bees, and which was as incomprehensible as the movie.

"Your homework is to ask your mothers to read this with you and give you 'The Talk,'" said my teacher, Mrs. Strange. More giggling ensued from my classmates who were in on the joke.

Mom looked irritated when I showed her the book after school. She flipped through the pages with a scowl. "Ugh. This looks like the same book they gave us in school when I was your age."

"For homework, you're supposed to read it with me and give me 'The Talk.'"

She groaned. "Maybe tomorrow." She went back to her typing.

I pestered her, day after day, until all the other girls in my class had reported to Mrs. Strange that they'd had The Talk with their mothers. Now they all knew things I didn't. I wasn't part of the inner circle of fifth-grade female wisdom. When all the boys in the class had had The Talk (presumably a different talk) with their fathers, everybody in the class was in on the joke except me.

After a week, Mom finally sat down with me for The Talk.

"Alright, Alice." She flipped through the book and put it down. "This is what you need to know. You're growing up, and pretty soon you'll start bleeding every month, and you'll have to wear sanitary napkins."

"Huh?"

I waited for further explanation. None was forthcoming. I started to cry.

"What's wrong, Honey?"

I cried harder and harder.

"Sweetie, what's the matter?"

I was convulsed in sobs. Mom hugged me.

"Alice, Sweetiepie, it's not so bad. It's just nature taking its course. You'll get used to it, I promise. Madeline gets her period. You can ask her about it. It's completely normal. My goodness, Alice, why are you so upset?"

"Where—" sob "—will I—" sob "—be bleeding—" sob "—from?"

"Where? Why, from . . . you'll bleed from your . . . private parts, of course."

"My *whaaaat*?" (Sob!)

"From . . . from your vagina."

"Oh." I wipe my nose on my shirt.

"You know what your vagina is, don't you?"

"Yeah, of course I do."

Vagina was one of the code words that made the girls giggle during the top-secret fifth-grade girl movie. I would look it up in our *Worldbook Encyclopedia*.

"What did you think I meant?"

"I thought you meant I'd be bleeding from everywhere."

"Oh dear!"

"I thought I'd be gushing blood from my entire body."

"Good heavens. No wonder you were upset." Mom held me closer.

"I thought that every month I'd have to wrap my whole body in napkins." I giggled through my tears. "Sanitary napkins—" I started to laugh "—like a mummy wrapped in really clean napkins."

Now, Mom was laughing with me. "I'm sorry, Sweetie. I'm no good at talking about this kind of thing. I admit that I'm kind of uptight about sex. I mean, talking about sex."

"That's okay, Mom." (Sex? Is that what we had just talked about?)

"Good. So we've had 'The Talk,' right?"

After The Talk, I still didn't know anything about sex. When my gullible little sister Jennifer (who believed everything I said) asked me, "What does mating mean?" I made an educated guess. "Mating is when a boy cat bites a girl cat's neck," I told her, while we spied on Amanda, as she lay down seductively in front of a virile tomcat and let him have his way with her.

Eliana reads silently, her mouth agape.

"*Ewww.* Did you and Daddy really do that?"

"Yup."

"Why didn't you ever tell me?"

"You never asked before."

I don't ask Eliana if she has any more questions. That's all I can handle for one afternoon.

Did I deal with Eliana's inquiries better than my mother did with mine? I hope so. In any event, this was light stuff, relatively speaking: *Motherhood 101.* Answering these inevitable childhood questions was a breeze, compared to the onerous maternal challenge that lies ahead—helping Eliana through her complicated and grueling medical ordeal. Have Michael and I adequately prepared her for what's going to happen? Is it better not to tell her too much? Will I have enough energy after my radiation treatment? How do I prepare, physically and emotionally, to help her?

I wish I could talk to my mother about it. Am I doing this right? For the first time in ages, Mom, I want to ask your advice—

Whoa, whoa, whoa! Where is this coming from? I was terrified when my mother appeared at my kitchen table the other day. Now I want to talk to her? I don't think so. I send thoughts in her general direction, somewhere in the stratosphere, trying to strike the right tone for addressing my mother's ghost—a balance of superstition and ironic detachment: Stay where you are. I repeat. Stay. Where. You. Are. Please, please, *please* don't show up again. *Tuh, tuh, tuh!* (I toss salt over my left shoulder for good measure.)

FIVE

Julia is home from an inspiring high school theater workshop at the Stratford Festival in Canada, where she was thrilled to perform Hamlet's "To be or not to be" soliloquy—a peak experience for a kid who's been enamored of Shakespeare since she was six years old, when I first took her to Shakespeare in the Park (a production of *Henry VIII*; hardly the Bard's most kid-friendly play, but Julia was spellbound.)

Radiant, confident, and relaxed, she's in full vacation mode, wearing a gauzy sundress, flip-flops and sunglasses, her waist-length thick brown hair sun-streaked with blonde, like it is every summer. She drops her suitcase and backpack in the living room. "It's good to be home." She reaches down and I reach up for a hug.

Next week is Julia's eighteenth birthday. She leaves for Princeton the week after that. These are our last days as a family of four living together under one roof. Julia didn't rebel in high school in that cataclysmic way you expect from adolescents. She's always been preternaturally good-natured and easy-going. But as soon as she got back from Canada, something must have kicked in. Her subconscious registered, "Oh, shit, I forgot to have my teenage rebellion! This is my last chance before I go to college." Consequently, she and I lock horns at least once a day. She's embarrassed by things I do (oh, for example, breathing). She lowers her eyelids in that way only a teenaged girl can do—that special, glowering look reserved for mothers—which makes me grumpy, so I try to glower back, but she's by far the superior glowerer. At six feet tall, she has the advantage of looking down at me when she glowers.

Julia can't wait to go to college. Another month at home and we'll both implode. I commit the cardinal sin of offering unsolicited suggestions. "Are you sure you should be drinking so much coffee?" I ask her, in our little kitchen. She ignores me, while brewing another pot for herself and Emily, her best friend since second grade. "Oh, never mind, your caffeine habit is excellent preparation for college life. Just promise me you won't join an eating club. Those elitist clubs are the last bastion of Princeton's old-boy privilege."

"Mom," she says with a teasing grin, putting her

hands on my shoulders and looking me straight in the eye, "I am planning to join an eating club. It's one of the things I'm looking forward to about Princeton."

"No, no, not the eating clubs! When I was in college, I joined a vegetarian cooking group and loved it."

"Really, Mom? That might have been cool when you were in college—in the *seventies*."

"*I'd* like to join a vegetarian cooking group," says Emily, reassuringly.

"Thank you, Emily."

Julia laughs. "Emily is a vegetarian and she goes to Hampshire College, so that doesn't count."

"I guess this is not your mother's Princeton," I sigh. The girls laugh.

A FEW DAYS after she gets back, Julia wakes at noon and asks if we can talk. We have the apartment to ourselves. Julia sits cross-legged on the sofa in the plaid boxer shorts and forest green tank top she wears as pajamas—her hair over one shoulder in a tousled, slept-in braid. I join her on the sofa, and she tells me, for the first time ever:

"Mom, I'm interested in finding my birth mother."

"Wow!"

"Yeah."

"That's wonderful," I say. And I mean it. I was at Julia's birth, and I fell in love with her birth mother, who was twenty at the time. Zoe didn't want to have any contact after the birth, but I always intuited that Julia would one day want to find her.

"This summer, for the first time in my life, I suddenly found myself wondering about Zoe, wanting to meet her. Being adopted didn't seem like a big deal for me growing up. I mean, this is my family. I always felt totally loved by you. And because you and I look so similar, people never assumed I was adopted, so that wasn't an issue."

Except for our height differences—she's six feet, I'm five feet three inches—Julia and I look uncannily like mother and daughter. We both have long, straight, brown hair, dark lashes and eyebrows, similar almond-shaped faces. Ever since she was a little girl, people have frequently said, "Julia, you look just like your mother," to which she politely agrees. If they ask, "Is your father tall?" she says, "Yes, he is." In fact, Julia's biological father is six feet seven inches. Ironically, I look more like my adopted daughter than my biological daughter. Eliana looks more like Michael.

"I'd love to help you with your search, Julia."

"Thanks, Mom. That means a lot to me."

It's something I've looked forward to since Julia was born. My memories of Zoe, and the family folklore we've shared with Julia about her, have been entirely positive. Julia wrote her college essay about her birth mother—about the gift Zoe gave her by choosing artists to be her adoptive parents, and what a huge influence the arts have had on her life. I want Julia to meet Zoe. Of course I do!

But today I hear her say "my birth mother" as if it's an entirely new concept. *Birth mother* is the thing I am not, was not, will never be for Julia. For the first time, the term *birth mother* makes me feel inadequate; a poor substitute, lacking in genetic credentials.

"Your timing is perfect, sweetheart. When you turn eighteen on Saturday, you can put your name in the National Adoption Registry, which helps reunite adopt-ees and birth parents. They might help you with your search—that is, if Zoe also chooses to register; a big *if*, but worth a try."

"Thanks, Mom. I'll do that eventually, but no rush."

"Understood." (That's a relief.)

"Right now I'm totally focused on college."

"Sure, Honey, that makes sense."

• • •

CLINGING TO OUR fleeting time as an intact family of four, I hastily organize a four-day weekend trip to Martha's Vineyard. I haven't been back to the Vineyard since my blissful summer job there, as arts director of the Chilmark Community Center, before my senior year in college. I have great memories of family vacations on the Vineyard as a kid. I want to share the island with my family.

Our minivacation is a total bust. Michael and I get stomach flu. We lie uselessly on our hotel bed and ask Julia to entertain her little sister. Julia is impatient to get home, see her friends, pack for college. Only Eliana is happy, hanging out with her awesome big sister, jumping in the waves, collecting shells, rescuing baby jellyfish that have washed ashore, making seaweed sculptures.

"I love it here! Can we come back to exactly the same place next summer?"

Michael groans. Julia rolls her eyes. I respond weakly from under the covers, "Sure, Sweetiepie, you and I will come back."

Monday morning, we catch the first ferry to the mainland. We're back home in New York City by mid-afternoon, Michael and I still wobbly.

I have surgery tomorrow.

And the play I've been working on is due the day after tomorrow. Repatriated to my desk in the living room after my feeble attempt at a beach escape, I turn on the computer. An e-mail from the producer reminds me, *"Email script by Wednesday. I want to consider* Oklahoma Samovar *for our season."*

I'm anxious about surgery. I'm anxious about Julia leaving for college. I'm anxious about the play. This never-ending play.

Oklahoma Samovar is a two-act, loosely based on the lives of my ancestors. My Latvian great-grandparents were the only Jews in the Oklahoma Land Run of 1889. It's a big play: two continents, a hundred years, three generations, commingling the past and present, the living and the dead; a cast of six actors playing two dozen roles.

I wrote the first draft of *Oklahoma Samovar* twenty years ago. I flew to Tulsa to interview my ancient Great Aunt Sylvia about the family history. Sylvia's big sister was Rose, my mother's mother. I never met Rose and had never even heard of Sylvia. I didn't know a thing about my Oklahoma roots, until my uncle filled me in, a few years after my mother's death.

My mother kept Oklahoma a secret.

Diminutive Aunt Sylvia had a photo on her dresser, in

a mother-of-pearl frame: a little girl in a white dress and a straw hat, standing by a peach tree.

"Ever seen this picture of your mama?" Sylvia asked in her high-pitched Oklahoma twang.

"No."

"Then it's yours, honey. Louise never told you 'bout us?"

"Nope."

"Why not?"

"I have no idea." I turned on my tape recorder. "Tell me everything, Sylvia."

"Oh, well, there's a lot to talk about, isn't there," she chuckled. "Where should I begin? My parents, Jake and Hattie—your great-grandparents—sailed to America from Latvia in 1887 when they were just seventeen years old. Jake came first, and Hattie followed. Jake drove a streetcar in New York City for a while, but he didn't like it one bit. When he found he could get a free plot of land in Kansas in exchange for plantin' three trees to show good intent to cultivate the land, why that's just what he did. Ya see, my daddy always had a mystical feelin' 'bout nature and workin' the land.

"When Hattie got off the boat, she thought Jake was still livin' in New York City, so she traipsed around the country, looking for Jake all over creation, carrying a feather bed and a samovar. It was her bridal trousseau. I still have that samovar, I'll show it to ya.

"Hattie finally caught up with Jake in Garden City, Kansas. Lord knows how she ever found him. 'Course there weren't any rabbis in Kansas at that time, so my parents were married by the banker, who was also the justice of the peace. They lived in a dirt dugout for two years. You see, there were no trees in the plains. Mama desperately wanted a wooden house and she wanted to cook on wood—she was plumb tired of cookin' on 'cow chips.'

"In 1889, they opened up the Oklahoma Territory. In order to get their hundred an' sixty acres of free land in Oklahoma, homesteaders had to *cut down* three trees, to show good intent to cultivate the land. Mama figured there'd be plenty wood in Oklahoma, so they left Kansas for the Oklahoma Land Run of 1889.

"Papa was missin' a thumb. He always told us it got blown off by a *sooner*—that's what they called the poachers at the Oklahoma Land Run, that crossed the startin' line *sooner* 'n they were s'posed to. Papa was the only Jew in the Land Run and the first peach farmer in Oklahoma Territory. The original homestead's still standin'. Your mother never told you 'bout the homestead?"

"Nope."

"Can't figure why not. Louise loved it here. She and I would go campin' together in a little cabin in the woods. She and I used to go huntin'."

"My mother hunted?"

"Yep. We'd shoot possum. Louise was good at it, too. *Heh-heh.* You sure she never told you about us?"

"Very sure."

"I wonder why."

"So do I."

Aunt Sylvia flew from Tulsa to see the premiere of *Oklahoma Samovar* two years later. She was so old, tiny, and frail that when I walked with her to the theater in the East Village, I feared the fierce November wind would carry her away. When the house lights faded and the performance began, Sylvia turned around to the man sitting behind her and proudly proclaimed, "That's *me* they're talkin' about! They're talkin' about *me*!"

In the play's first incarnation, I hadn't yet figured out the story I wanted to tell. Each reading launched a new set of rewrites. A year ago, my friend Eric directed a workshop production of the play, which illuminated some questions and raised new ones. My mother is now a character in the play, a fictionalized version of her as an eight-year-old in 1929. I wonder if the play needs to be more about my mother or less about her. Now that she's been showing up at my kitchen table, maybe I should ask her—*ha!*

How can I possibly finish this rewrite in two days?

As I read through the script, scribbling notes, the phone rings. It's my ex-husband, calling from his home in L.A.

"Hi, Brad."

"Alice, are you sitting down?"

"Yes."

"I found Zoe!"

"What?"

"I looked her up on the Internet, and she has a website, so I—"

"Wait. WHAT? You. Go back. You *found* Zoe?"

"Yes."

"What do you mean *found*? How did you—"

"I just got off the phone with her a minute ago! She has—"

"You *called* her?"

"Her phone number is on her website. She wants to see Julia. She has two baby girls, she's married—"

"But what about Zoe's—"

"Her husband knows all about the adoption. Zoe wants to see Julia! I'd like to tell Julia myself."

"Sure. Um. Would you mind waiting till tomorrow to tell her?"

"Okay. Absolutely. Isn't this great news?"

"Yes . . . wow. She wants to see . . . That's . . . that's fantastic news."

So why am I so angry?

After Brad hangs up, I slam down the receiver, put my face in my hands and groan. In my roiling tumult and turmoil about mothers and birth mothers—about Julia looking for her birth mother, about Brad preemptively finding Zoe, about mothers lost and found—I want to find *my* mother. Where's the National Registry that will facilitate my search? Sign me up. Heck, I'll just Google her. Maybe she has a website with her phone number on it. Ha!

With my face in my hands, I say her name out loud— Mom . . . Mommy . . . Louise.

"Why are you so angry, Alice," she asks, inside my head. *(This time, it's just my mother's voice. Not a visitation. That's okay.)*

"Because, in one move, Brad has (1) usurped Julia's

quest to find her birth mother; (2) violated Zoe's privacy. Zoe wanted anonymity. We weren't even supposed to know her last name. And, oh, for example, what if Zoe had *not* told her husband, and what if she did *not* want him to know she'd given up a baby for adoption eighteen years ago? And (3) he left me out of the process. I wanted to help Julia with her search."

"Of course you did."

"And now—Anyway, it's done."

"True. Brad can't un-find Zoe."

"I know that this is great news. I'm being petulant and petty. And that's the worst thing, Mom. I'm ashamed. I want to be a better mother than that."

"Your feelings are completely understandable, especially in context."

"What context?"

"Julia leaving home on Saturday."

"Ouch, don't remind me."

"And your surgery is tomorrow."

"Right. Ugh. I'm really scared, Mom. Mommy, I am. I'm really, really scared."

"You'll be fine."

"How do you know?"

"I don't."

"Then why'd you say I'd be fine?"

"That's what we mothers say."

"Whether or not it's true?"

"We comfort our children. It's part of the job. Anyway, your surgery isn't such a big deal."

"Not like yours, you mean?"

"Good luck tomorrow, Alice—*tuh, tuh, tuh!* Be sure to throw salt over your left shoulder."

SIX

. . . .

Michael is there when I awaken from the anesthesia, my left breast smaller by a peach-sized lump of flesh than it was when I woke up that morning. I insist on walking the fifteen blocks home, even though I stumble out of the hospital in a groggy daze. Michael puts his arm around my shoulder and helps me to navigate the sidewalks and traffic lights on the steamy day. I zigzag drunkenly, hugging an ice pack under my shirt to reduce the swelling. I'm sore from the procedure, but I no longer have shooting pains. I'm infinitely grateful that the metal marker was removed, as promised. I desperately want coffee. Michael ushers me into a Starbucks, buys me a monumental cup of dark brew, and walks me home.

I look at myself in the bedroom mirror. The asymmetry of my breasts gives the pair a cock-eyed look. It amuses me.

I remember my mother's body, when it was beautiful.

At three years old, I would play on the floor in the warm, steamy bathroom while Mom took a shower, her curvy silhouette visible through the translucent vinyl shower curtain. She turns off the water, opens the shower curtain, and reaches for the white towel. I look up to admire her large, round breasts as she leans over me, eclipsing the ceiling lamp, steam emanating from her body like a halo of light. She dries herself, wraps the towel around her chest. She's so young, much younger than I am now, lovely and sexy. My breasts are the same size and shape as hers were. Except that my left one is now a little smaller.

I WAKE UP early the next day to make eleventh-hour revisions to *Oklahoma Samovar,* typing slowly with one hand, holding an ice pack in the other. It hurts, but I skip the pain meds, because they make me sleepy.

As five p.m. approaches, I type FINAL DRAFT on the cover page. Have I actually finished it?

My finger hovers over the keyboard for an inordinately long time.

I hit send. I sit with the finality of it.

I wait for a sense of euphoria.

Fulfillment? I'd settle for contentment.

Instead, I feel deeply unsettled. Why? Don't I want the

play to be finished? I've been working on it for such a long time. Could it be that I'm not ready to end my relationship with it? Maybe writing this fictionalized story of Mom's family is my way of searching for my mother. Working on it all these years kept her with me, and hitting *send* is sending her away.

I'm troubled by a vestigial belief that I'm not allowed to complete it, that I've betrayed my mother's tradition of working on a book forever and never finishing.

Is that it? Are you mad at me, Mom? Envious that I finished my play, even though it took me twenty years?

Are you angry because my cancer isn't as bad as yours was? Do you resent that I have it easy, just a simple lumpectomy? That my cancer is stage zero and entirely curable, whereas yours disfigured and almost killed you?

Or am I unsettled because my breast hurts?

"Mom," says Julia, startling me.

"Oh! Hi, Honey, I didn't hear you come in."

She's fresh from a shower, wrapped in a white terrycloth robe and brushing her wet hair.

"Are you busy?"

"No. As a matter of fact, I just this minute finished the play I've been working on for—well, forever, it seems—so I'm done for the day." I take off my reading glasses and emphatically close my laptop, to illustrate how *not* busy I am.

"How are you feeling, Mom?"

"Good. I mean. Only okay. Pretty sore, actually."

"Can I get you a new ice pack? That one's melted."

"Ah, so it is. Thank you, that would be lovely."

I try to get comfortable on the sofa, propping myself up with strategically placed throw pillows. Julia hands me a new ice pack, which provides some relief. She sits across from me and folds her long legs under her. Her face brims with an emotion I can't identify.

"What's on your mind, sweetheart?"

"Did my dad mention to you that he found Zoe?"

"Yes, he did. I'm so excited for you. How do you feel about it? Do you want to contact her?"

Julia parts her lips, about to answer, pauses, grins, takes a deep breath. "Actually, I talked to Zoe on the phone last night."

"What. Um. Wow! I. You already called her. You. Wow. Wha-wha-what? Did—Wow," I babble, rendered temporarily incoherent, "Wow. What was it like?"

"It was really great!'

Ouch! I'm losing Julia. I've pushed her away and now she's found another mother. Her first mother. She leaves for college in two days. She's so out of here. I was so focused on taking care of Eliana's needs that I nearly forgot about Julia. What have I done?

"We friended each other on Facebook."

"Really?

"Yeah." Julia is glowing.

"That's amazing. That's—"

FRIENDED ON FACEBOOK!

Finding one's birth mother is supposed to be an Epic Quest. Call me old-fashioned, but I thought there would be some weight to the search, gravitas to the moment of connection. The archetypal reunion. Facebook? Too easy. But given Julia and Zoe's shared proclivity for smooth-sailing serenity, this was precisely their kind of quest.

Adopting wasn't easy. The two-year adoption process had plenty of pitfalls. As Julia grew up, I anticipated that her search for her birth mother would have all the Odyssean tasks that inevitably accompany quests. That's how I'd always imagined it. . . . Okay, so Julia isn't me. She's part Zoe. Zoe is breezy and light-hearted, as is Julia. I should rejoice. Being neither breezy nor light-hearted myself, this isn't easy for me.

Oh, and I should mention that Julia doesn't want to "friend" me. Which is totally *fine* with me. I don't need to be my teenage daughter's Facebook friend. I don't care. (Not until, like, this minute, when I desperately want to be one of Julia's thousand-plus "friends.") I'm not jealous. Yes, I am. I'm *so* jealous.

Julia gets her laptop from the dining table, and returns to the sofa, snuggling up next to me with the computer on her lap.

"Look at this, Mom."

Julia, beaming, shows me photos on Zoe's Facebook page. "Doesn't Zoe's baby look exactly like me as a baby? Isn't she adorable?"

"Yes, she does look like you, and yes, she's adorable."

Zoe is still youthful-looking at age thirty-eight, with her handsome husband and their two very cute little girls, who both resemble Julia.

My ambivalence about Julia's joy at finding her birth mother is interfering with my goal of being an exemplary mother. I have to try harder. Everything is topsy-turvy. Julia is now the age Zoe was when she gave birth to Julia. Zoe is the age I was when I adopted Julia. It's confusing.

Why are both of our long-lost mothers suddenly back in our lives right now, after such a long absence? Of course, Julia's birth mother is alive, and my mother is, well—

"Zoe invited me to visit her in Florida and meet her family some time in the next year."

"Wow, that's great, sweetheart!"

But it's not all great. Why have I been so eager to see Julia off to college? I miss her already.

"Thanks for being so supportive, Mom. It means the world to me."

"Of course, of course, it's incredible, its, it's, it's . . . Can I take you out to celebrate? Right now, this minute?"

"Aw, thanks, but I'm about to have a picnic in the park with Emily and a few of our friends, and then we're going to a party downtown." She glances at the clock and gets up. "I should get dressed."

"Then how about the four of us go out to dinner tomorrow night," I ask, sounding a little more desperate than I'd intended. "Our last night together before you go to college."

"That sounds excellent."

Why can't I admit to myself how much I love my children and how much I miss them when they are gone? This is the recurrent theme this summer. I want to be a great mother, but I keep tripping myself up. The harder I try to be a good mother, the more I'm haunted by being a daughter.

WHEN WE ARRIVE at Princeton, Julia seems instantly at home. College is a perfect fit. At freshman registration, she registers to vote in New Jersey. She's recruited for Women's Crew. "You're the perfect size for rowing," the coach tells Julia, the only six-foot-tall freshman girl in the gymnasium.

My breast hurts and I don't feel well, so I wait in the lobby of Julia's dorm while Michael, Julia, and Eliana haul her stuff up to the room. I gingerly hug Julia goodbye. On the drive back to the city, I remember the day Mom and Dad brought me to Princeton and helped me carry my stuff into the dorm. I couldn't wait to leave home that summer, but when Mom and Dad drove away that first day, I was terribly homesick and lonely—that is, until a very handsome boy invited me to join a game of Frisbee in the courtyard.

I WAKE EARLY the next morning, feeling horrible. My left breast is burning hot. Turns out I have a staph infection. In the days following, I lie in bed with a high fever, popping antibiotics and Advil, alternating between fever dreams and TV, which isn't much better than the fever dreams; the Republican Convention has begun.

I have one of those resistant staph infections, so my

doctor switches me to industrial strength antibiotics, big as horse pills. I can't start radiation until the infection is cured. I'm slightly delirious, sweating and shivering in bed.

Michael takes Eliana to her first day of fourth grade. My fever is down, but I'm wiped out, still recuperating at home. The house seems so quiet with both of my girls gone. I get out of bed and pad around in my nightgown and slippers. Harry Potter the Hamster finishes his aerobic workout on the squeaky running wheel. He stuffs his cheeks with food and carries it to his bedroom, fluffs up his bedding, surrounds himself with food, and goes to sleep for the day. It's an enviable plan.

I notice an old wooden cigar box on top of the bookshelf. I'd forgotten about it. My father gave it to me years ago. Inside is a stack of my mother's letters—the paper yellowed and crumbling. I've never read them before. It's all that's left of Mom's writing. After she died, we tossed out cartons of her papers, thousands of pages. In our rush to mourn and move on, we threw away nearly everything she ever wrote.

I carefully unfold a letter my Mom wrote in 1942, when she was a Columbia grad student. It's addressed to Matt, a lieutenant in Fort Sill, Oklahoma. I guess Matt never got this letter—not this draft, anyway. The typed letter is covered with Mom's hand-written cross-outs and edits.

April 18, 1942

Dear Matt,

I officially grew up last week. I was twenty-one on the 11th . . . Was quite surprised at your attitude towards women going 'out into the world.' It never occurred to me to doubt that I would do otherwise. Though there have been many a time that I felt I was attempting to cut across insurmountable feminine instincts for cooking, sewing, home-making and the like.

What I should really like to do is go to some wild woody place in the North West and seriously go in for farming. I think there's something very satisfying about working on the land. One can see the logical results of one's efforts. Besides I have some sort of mystical love of the outdoors. At any rate, it isn't up to us women to decide. We have to take on these new responsibilities.

The letter is both clarifying and mystifying. My mother was always a feminist ahead of her time, always wrestling with the contradictions between her ambitions and external rules and expectations. But farming? I guess she had some of her grandfather Jake in her. And, I wonder, did she ever go out into the world—*"It never occurred to me that I would do otherwise"*—in the way she always thought she would?

In a 1942 letter to her brother Edwin, then in officer training school, she wrote:

Dear Edwin . . . Last term I was really quite blue. I found myself drifting. But this term, all the bits of driftwood seem to be coming together and forming a most interesting pattern. All my work is beginning to dovetail. My public administration study forms the basis for analyzing planning problems, and sociology and general political science gives such analysis a valid and rounded foundation. I'm beginning to get a working methodology, a substantial frame of reference.

This sounds like Mom. Periods of unhappy brooding, leavened by intellectual euphoria, diving headlong into her work. I guess the pattern was imprinted at an early age.

A 1945 journal entry reads,

Sunday A.M.—Gloomy, unhappy. This idea of having three men in the space of two days converge and propose was too much. I should have been thrilled, but no feeling of elation. People's emotions are delicate but powerful . . .

After a bond of intimacy or friendship has been established it is difficult to break it off.

Moving forward in time, her letters as a young mother probe the depths of "housewifely melancholia" and suburban life.

Jan 20, 1959

Dear George and Beryl: How muddy this type is—obviously my typewriter is not primed for creative effort—nor my mind either. It's been snowing fitfully today, that sloshy, sleety indeterminate way it has of doing here—and the sogginess of the outside has mingled with the interior mood of our household. It is in fact the kind of day when I should have liked to commune with Beryl—and probe the depths of housewifely melancholia. But this is dispelled now—these acid yellow sheets of yours have charged the atmosphere. I am agog with the splendor of your life in Washington.

And ten months later:

Oct 10, 1959

Dear George and Beryl: I can hardly wait the arrival of those dark, cozy, early evenings when the children and the supper can be packed up and off at a reasonable hour. This

summer has been so diffuse. The baby was impossible to
contain and there was never a moment's rest from her insa-
tiable and ferocious drive to wander outside and away. . . .
The summer at home was incredibly busy with children.
What a rare delight when school began—Alice is in kinder-
garten now. Playground hours in our backyard are now
only after school.

I feel momentarily crushed, on Jennifer's behalf as well
as my own. *"A rare delight when school began—Alice*
is in kindergarten." She couldn't wait to get me out of
the house; she was undone by baby Jennifer's insatiable
exploring.

And yet, why wouldn't she be? Haven't I always been
the same with my daughters? From Julia's first days of
preschool, I craved those precious child-free hours from
nine a.m. to three p.m. when I could get back to my work,
focus on the stuff of my adult life that was important to
me. That's exactly how I felt this morning, immensely
relieved that both girls were back at school and I finally
had the apartment to myself.

But when I hear my mother's 1959 sigh of relief, from
this time capsule of letters, I feel a sharp jab, a remembered wound, an unrelieved longing: me wanting my
mother more than she wanted me.

Would I have preferred for her to conform to the fifties

paradigm of a housewife and mother, single-mindedly dedicated to her children? Not now, now that I know better. And did that paradigm even exist outside of our black-and-white television set, or was it a fabrication designed to dissuade our mothers from "going out into the world"? But when I was a little kid, brought up on *Leave it to Beaver* sitcom family values, then yeah, sure, it seemed like the way things should be.

"What should we get Mommy for Mother's Day?" Dad asked my sisters and me.

"How about a brand-new broom and dustpan?"

"Yeah, a brand-new broom and dustpan," we all agreed. As soon as we got home from the store, we ran into the kitchen where Mom was preparing lunch. "Happy Mother's Day!" we shouted, handing her the gift—the unwrapped broom and dustpan, tied together at the neck with a red ribbon.

She stared at it for a moment, let it drop loudly to the floor, and stormed out of the room in disgust. There was no laugh track to our blunder. We stared dumbly at the broom and dustpan on the floor, a collective thought bubble of slow recognition forming over our four heads.

My fever is down. The infection is finally over.

Michael and I make love that night. I ask him to try not to touch my left breast, which is still sore. He lavishes attention on my right breast, to compensate. I love that.

"Do you mind the scar, Michael?"

"I don't notice it."

I love that, too.

I start radiation next week. I won't need chemo, and that's a huge relief.

After Michael falls asleep, I stand naked in front of the bedroom mirror. My left breast, deflated by surgery, then inflated by infection, is back to its original size. The scar is healed, barely visible. I feel good. I'm grateful my body wasn't scarred by cancer, the way my mother's was. I wonder if my daughters worried about that. Did they have a vision of me disfigured by surgery? I shudder, suddenly asking myself, What if my daughters' beautiful bodies were some day ravaged by disease? What if Eliana's leg-lengthening surgery injures rather than heals her?

I've never told my girls what my mother went through.

I picture my mother, naked. Her breasts are gone. Her bony chest is crisscrossed with long, red scars, like uneven train tracks. Her armpits are carved out, where the lymph nodes were removed. Her face is etched with sadness, anger, resentment, and envy. That's how she looked at me—after her surgery, after my loving and exuberant mother was replaced by a gloomy, gray ghost of herself. These are the parts that frightened me when I was a teenager and made me hate her, the parts I've always tried to forget. When I was twelve and just starting to develop, Mom's damaged body terrified me. When I picture her today, her scarred body looks heroic, sad but strangely beautiful. Now, I wish I could make amends for shutting her out.

THE MUSICIANS SIT on the Persian rug covering the wide window seat. The long-necked, turbaned sitar player improvises a mind-bogglingly complex raga on his long-necked instrument, which he balances between his left foot and right knee; while the compact, black-haired tabla player extracts intricate rhythms from his two drums, varying the pitch with the heel of his hand.

My mother and I sit at a table near the duo, enthralled by the music and by the plates of food passing by. Mom is ancient, white-haired, wrinkled and bony, but surprisingly animated. She's wearing a white nightgown and she's barefoot, which seems to fit in at this restaurant—maybe because the musicians are also barefoot and dressed in white. The slim young waiter glides as if on wheels, delivering aromatic dishes to other customers—steamy curries, sizzling tandoori platters, deep-fried pakoras, and puffy golden poori bread. Invisible tendrils of coriander, cumin, cloves, and cinnamon waft by our table. Each intoxicating spice has a particular sound and a color—a note that harmonizes with the music and a hue that blends with the red and marigold walls, the purple upholstery, the copper statues of Hindu gods.

"The music is so glorious, I feel guilty talking," my mother whispers, leaning across the table. "Mmmm, everything looks and smells so delicious. I love this restaurant."

"We came here once, a long time ago."

"Did we? I don't remember. It's all a blur."

"Yeah . . . Mom, there's so much I want to tell you."

"Well, here I am," she says, and in slow motion she stands up and extends her arms, like an eagle spreading her wings—or maybe a scrawny angel. The musicians match her tempo and slow down the music as she opens herself up, as if this is meant to be a dance accompanied by tabla and sitar. The gown's flimsy fabric reveals the angular contours of her rib cage and the loose skin drooping from her bony arms. "Here I am, Honeylamb. This is your chance to tell me anything."

Then she drops into her chair, exhausted by the effort. Slumped over, she rests her arms on the table and catches her breath. The musicians pick up the tempo, and she perks up.

"Mom, I wish that you could have met my daughters, and my husband—and that they could have met you."

"Oh, goodness, yes, it's a shame we never met." She sits straighter. "From everything I've observed, my granddaughters are amazing girls, so different, one from the other, and yet both of them smart and kind and imaginative and brave—truly courageous, each in her own way. And Michael. You chose a wonderful man, Sweetheart, which is a laudable triumph. He's one of the good ones. A gem."

"Wow, I'm glad you think so. You didn't like *any* of my boyfriends."

"That was then. I'm sure I wasn't easy to live with."

"No. I guess I wasn't, either."

"Nope. Now where did that waiter go? I'm starving."

"I'm sorry, Mom, for so many things."

"Well, choose one thing and get it over with, Sweetheart, so we can order dinner."

"I'm sorry we gave you that stupid broom and dustpan on Mother's Day."

PART 2

"It's not true, yes it's true, it's true and
it's not true, there is silence and there is not
silence, there is no one and there is someone,
nothing prevents anything."

—SAMUEL BECKETT,
Stories and Texts for Nothing

ONE

"I loved having radiation," says Aunt Phyllis, my father's sister, my fairy godmother, my good luck charm, my surrogate mom—the optimist I wish I could be.

"I don't believe you, Phyl. Nobody loves radiation."

"Well, *I* did! Listen to me, dahling. It was almost thirty years ago, but I'll never forget. Arthur had just died, and I was getting used to being alone for the first time in my life. When my doctor told me I would have to go every day for six weeks, I thought I'd be bored to death. So I decided to add a little variety. I drove to the hospital a different route every day. It was like seeing my neighborhood for the first time. The leaves were changing color. Oh, it was the most beautiful fall. I know it sounds crazy, Alice, but I loved radiation. I missed it when it was over."

"That's impossible. Nobody misses radiation."

"*I* did. I loved the whole experience."

I keep Phyllis's reminiscence as a mantra. As if I could ever love it. But who knows.

"You'll start Monday," says Dr. Sofia Giordano, my elegant and erudite radiologist, in a lilting Italian accent. "Thirty sessions, five days a week for six weeks. Today, we design your treatment plan."

The technician applies permanent tattoos to my back—four small black dots that I'll have for the rest of my life—and aligns a laser grid to the dots to capture 3-D images. Before allowing me to move, she marks the position of my tumor with a big X, drawn with blue magic marker.

"Don't wash off the X. It has to last the weekend."

X Marks the Spot. Like a pirate's treasure map. Or an executioner's document. Or my mother's lullaby. *X marks the spot, with a dot, dot, dot.*

It's my first day. The hour-long commute begins with a rush-hour subway from Seventy-second Street, mashed into a standing-room-only train, followed by the walk west through the crush of midtown crowds. I pause outside the NYU Cancer Institute on Thirty-fourth Street and Third Avenue. Radiation scares me. My instinct is to "duck and cover," to hide under a desk like we did in kindergarten in 1959, in the deluded belief that this would protect us from radioactive fallout, should an atomic bomb explode in the vicinity of our classroom. In the waiting room, surrounded by fellow cancer patients— my new peers—I try to channel Aunt Phyllis's optimism: My cancer is stage zero and completely curable. I'm incredibly lucky. (Oops, don't tempt the Evil Eye. *Tuh, tuh, tuh!*)

"My name is Jamal," says a velvety and masculine, Caribbean-accented voice, rousing me from my prayer of gratitude. "This is Reggie. You can come in now."

Jamal is from Barbados, Reggie is from Brooklyn. Jamal is tall and muscled, Reggie is short and slight. They are both dark-skinned and handsome. I like these guys. I take off my robe and lie face down on a foam mattress with a hole cut out for my left breast to hang down, so that my heart and lung will be out of the line of fire when I'm nuked. I'm surprisingly unselfconscious about being naked from the waist up. The mattress is lined with the softest cotton sheets. The room is chilly. Reggie covers me with a warmed sheet. Jamal lays a heated blanket over my feet. Nice.

"Just relax," says Jamal. "Don't try to help us position you."

Reggie and Jamal move me incrementally right and left, gently pushing and pulling my shoulders, arms, waist, back, ribs. Like a minimal massage, sort of sexy. I ask myself whether it's ethical to sexually enjoy being handled by these gorgeous and (I assume) straight guys. Under the circumstances, why not enjoy the absurd sensuality of it?

"Don't move until we say so," says Reggie, smoothing the sheet over my shoulders.

Reggie and Jamal close the padded door behind them.

"Stay absolutely still for ten minutes," says Jamal over the loudspeaker. "Radiation is commencing."

THE WALLS ARE gray, the lights are dim. A Handel symphony is barely audible over the fan and the intermittent electronic beeps and drones. I survey the room as much as I can with my left cheek pressed to the mattress.

The radiation machine is a sleek robot, about seven feet tall, steely gray curves. A pivoting metal arm is the only movement in the room, precisely aiming radiation beams from many directions. It circles above me, pauses; circles to the right of me, pauses; circles below me, pauses; circles to my left, pauses. "Do not breathe so deeply," says Jamal over the speaker. "It makes your chest rise and fall too much, and the radiation will miss its mark. Just breathe normally."

Breathing deeply is normal for me—thanks to all those years of clarinet lessons in my youth and yoga classes as an adult—so it's an effort to *not* breathe deeply. Shallow breathing does not feel normal. I have to Zen the anti-Zen-ness of it.

Ten minutes is a long time to stay absolutely still.

A loose hair tickles my nose each time I inhale and exhale. For each one of six hundred seconds, it flutters over my nostril, and all I can think about is the hair, my itchy nose, and my fear of radiation, all of which conspire to make the minutes feel interminable. My back muscle seizes up. *Aarrgh*. Ouch. Itchy nose, sore back, itchy nose, sore back, nose, back, nose, fuck . . .

"YOU MAY MOVE about now, Ms. Cohen."

. . .

How could Aunt Phyllis have loved radiation?

What would Phyllis do? She took a different route to her radiation treatments every morning, and watched the leaves change color. I'll give it a try.

The next day, I drop Eliana off at school before my appointment. Her friend Jojo runs up to her, and they skip into the building, arms linked, whispering and giggling. I forego the subway, walk to Central Park, and enter the Ramble, a serenely beautiful wooded area with winding paths, tall boulders, and hidden ponds. The traffic noise drops away. My ears ring in this unaccustomed quiet. Bird calls, the wind rustling through branches, a squirrel spiraling rapidly down a tree. The leaves are just beginning to change. A bright red cardinal streaks by. I breathe deeply, inhaling the smell of dry leaves and crisp fall air. I didn't realize I'd been so nature-deprived. When I arrive at my appointment, my body is warm, perspiring, loosened up. My lungs have had an expansive hour to limber up for their daily ten-minute regime of shallow breathing.

I lie still, head turned to the right, left cheek on the sheet. With my peripheral vision, I follow the ascent of the metal arm of the radiation machine, making her silent arabesque, circling me in her strange dance. The bed itself now approaches the machine, as if she were an enormous octopus, pulling me toward her with her one long tentacle, to hold me in her maternal embrace, or to squeeze the life out of me. I soften my vision, listen to my breath, the fan, the mechanical beeps, a Mozart string quartet.

Time stands still.

Beep, beep, beep.

Mom. Mommy. Louise. She's here.

I tried so hard not to think about her, for such a long time. Now she's right in front of my eyes. I can't even turn my head to look away; I'm not allowed to move for ten minutes. My young, beautiful mother is standing beside the radiation bed, so close to me that I feel the warmth radiating from her body and her breath on my face—more vivid and tangible than any flashback.

Memories flood into the space left empty for thirty years. I don't resist. I want my mother with me. At this moment I don't need to be a mother, I just want to be a daughter. I need her right now. For the first time in decades, I want to remember everything about her. She holds out her hand. I reach for her, sliding my fingers over the threshold of her palm. With a crackle of electricity, her hand envelopes mine, and we tumble and swirl in a rush and roar of wind, traveling out of the room and back in time.

I held Mommy's hand, trying to keep up with her. I was five years old.

"Come with me, Alice."

Madeline had to stay home to take care of Jennifer, who was only two. Campaigning for Civil Rights with Mom was a privilege. This was my first time. I felt my face blush. I wanted her to be proud of me. We went door to door. It was a warm summer evening, before dinnertime and the evening news, and she walked fast in her clippity cloppity high heels.

Knock knock knock.

We waited outside the door. I looked up at my mother. She smiled at me and squeezed my hand. She looked like a movie star, with red lips and shiny black curls, wearing the blue dress Daddy gave her on her birthday, the one he said gave her a good figure. She looked like Jackie Kennedy, from on television, except Mom was in color.

Knock knock knock.

"Oh, it's you. Mrs. *Cohen.* What do you want?" said a man, opening the door halfway.

"Would you sign this petition and support antisegregation legisla—"

Bang! Door slammed in Mom's face. Why did he do that? It was rude.

She gripped my hand tighter. "C'mon, Alice." She pulled me faster than before. "This is important work, Sweetheart." The way she said that made me feel so special that I blushed again. We got to the next house on the block.

Knock knock knock.

"What do *you* want, Louise?" said a wife.

"Hi, Jeannie, how are you?" said my mother.

"Who is that?" called a man's voice, from deeper inside the house.

"It's Louise *Cohen,*" said the wife.

I didn't like the way the neighbors said *Cohen.*

"She's here with her petition again. What should I do?"

"Tell her we're not interested," said the husband's voice.

"Why aren't they interested?" I asked, when the door had closed.

"I don't know," she said, her voice grumpy.

At the next house, a girl from my school peeked from behind her mother's legs. I was too shy to say hi or anything in the seconds before the door was shut.

One woman said, "Sure, Louise, sign me up. I don't know too much about it, but I'll sign," and she did, and she and Mom chatted for a while. I was glad she signed it and talked with my mom, even though her cigarette was smelly. Mom shook her head no at me for holding my nose, and it was time to leave.

At the next house, the word "Jew" snaked through the door in a hissing whisper, in the millisecond before it slammed.

And so on, to all the doors around the block.

Then we walked back to our house on Wilbur Avenue. Even though we had only gone around our block, it felt like we'd traveled a long way. I was tired. So was she, I could tell.

"Don't ever give up, Sweetheart," she said when we got home, kneeling down so she was eye level with me, putting both hands on my shoulders. "Even when it's frustrating, you have to speak up for what you believe is right."

"Okay, Mom." I liked it when she looked me in the

eye and said serious things to me, stuff I'd have to remember forever and ever.

Then I ran into the living room to play with my sisters and Amanda the Cat. Madeline was practicing guitar, so I went outside with Jennifer, who was finally old enough to be fun to play with. We ran around in the backyard, and I pushed her on the swing. Kevin from across the street sneaked up on us and called her "Baby, Baby," in a mean voice, which made her cry, so I shouted, "When you're two, you're not a baby anymore, dummy!" Somehow, that shut Kevin up and he slunk away. Jennifer stopped crying and looked up at me like I was her hero.

When my father came home from work, Madeline and Jennifer and I ran to greet him. Hugs all around, Daddy swinging us in the air, youngest to oldest. My mom brought in a plate of crackers and cheddar cheese, celery and carrots and V8 juice, and we had to be quiet while Daddy smoked a cigar and watched the evening news, and Mom made dinner. The cigar smelled yucky, but we weren't allowed to tell him that.

We sat down to eat baked chicken, mashed potatoes, and creamed spinach. Mommy used big words to tell Daddy about her day, about the class she taught at City University. I didn't understand the words, *"Designation of class . . . A mosaic of identities . . . The insulation of life in suburbia . . . ,"* but the overall effect was like listening to music. *"Juxtaposition of wealth and poverty . . ."* Shimmering syllables streamed from her mouth, like notes and melodies, *"An intricate and precise patterning . . ."* as fast as the rippling Chopin arpeggios Daddy played on the piano.

She told him about her research for the paper she was writing. *"The unwritten covenants of discrimination . . . A conspiracy of silent acceptance . . ."* Daddy, who loved his dinner, answered while chewing, with approving grunts, "Unh. Mmm," and some medium-sized words, "Great, Louise. That's marvelous." But she did most of the talking. *"Myriad municipalities . . . Economic and color barricades around their boundaries . . . Varying strata of the community . . . Catholic, Protestant, Jewish, Negroes . . ."*

After red jello and whipped cream, Madeline, Jennifer, and I cleared the table. My mother washed the dishes, while my father played the piano in the living room. I played hide and seek with Jennifer. Madeline had just turned ten and had lots of friends. She was tired of playing with me, because I wouldn't be six till November.

When Mom finished cleaning the kitchen and putting

Jennifer to bed, she sat down at her typewriter, slipped off her shoes, and stretched her legs. I sat next to her, kicked off my shoes, and wiggled my toes. The stack of discarded pages—translucent onionskin paper with Mom's red ballpoint pen cross-outs, and waxy carbon copies with pale blue ink—belonged to me.

"Can you draw quietly, so I can concentrate?"

"Okay, Mommy."

"Thanks, Sweetheart."

Typing, typing, typing.

"What are you writing?"

"A book."

"What's it called?"

She sighed audibly, which meant she was annoyed that I interrupted her.

"What's your book called?"

"'My PhD Dissertation.'" *Tappitty, tappitty, tappity.*

"That's a silly name," I giggled. "What does 'Pea Aichdy Dish of Tashin' mean?"

She kept working, didn't answer, so I picked up a crayon and drew a picture on the back of a page covered with her words, some scribbled over with ballpoint pen, a mosaic of words and arrows.

Mom used so many big words, I was accustomed to

not knowing what she meant. I sat beside her, drawing and drawing, Mommy typing and typing. She paused.

"What are you drawing?"

"A picture of you, Mommy."

"I love it!"

TWO

I love that Eliana still likes holding hands when we walk to school. Julia had given it up by this age.

"Mom, why can't I walk to school by myself?"

"Because you're too young."

"I'm in fourth grade, I'm not a baby!" She withdraws her hand. "Some kids in my class already walk to school alone. When can I walk to school on my own?"

"Um . . ."

What's the point in letting her walk to school alone now, when in one month she'll have surgery and then she won't be able to walk to school at all, with or without me? What's the point of giving her more independence now, only to take it away from her? *And* I don't think she's ready.

"At the end of fifth grade. That's when Julia was allowed to walk to school alone."

"Okay." She takes my hand again, and skips the rest of the way to school. I veer off eagerly, to walk through the park and to my session.

Walking home from first grade, I thought about God, and wondered whether our God was the same as the God that Kevin and Sally believed in. How could it be the same God, since Sally said that when they died they'd be angels in God's heaven but we couldn't ever go there, because we were Jewish and the Jews killed Christ, and that was why we couldn't ever be saved. Their heaven sounded comfortable, with good music on harps, but rather snobby and mean. It reminded me of the sailing club Daddy wanted to join, but they wouldn't let him because Jews weren't allowed.

My parents weren't specific on the subject of death and angels and heaven and God, and we only went to synagogue twice a year, on Rosh Hashanah and Yom Kippur, and it was mostly in Hebrew, which I didn't understand. Mom said she didn't believe in an afterlife. Dad said he was agnostic, but he wasn't ruling anything out. Mom said she believed in reincarnation, which sounds pretty cool, like maybe you'd come back in your next life as a lion, which was my favorite animal. But when I pressed her for details, she said she believed that when your body was buried, it helped plants to grow, which sounded boring. Mom and Dad both said it was okay to believe whatever seemed right to you. I hadn't worked out the details (like my dad, I wasn't ruling anything out), but I thought that whatever you believed was true, and that there were many heavens and many Gods, even though everyone said theirs was the only one. Kevin and Sally would probably go to their heaven that had no Jews in it, because they were so certain about it, and I'd go to the other heaven that lets in Jews. But what if I believed my heaven was for everybody? Then Kevin and Sally would be there, too. Phooey, that meant Kevin would still throw rocks at me in heaven. But maybe they wouldn't even know we were in the same heaven, and then wouldn't I have the last laugh? Just like Daddy said he had the last laugh when he won the sailing championship last summer even though he wasn't allowed to join the yacht club.

Eliana sleepily sits down to breakfast in blue and red striped pajamas, her unruly caramel hair an appealing mess. I arrange scrambled eggs, sliced cantaloupe, and toast on her plate, and open the fridge to make her lunch.

"I miss Julia," she says.

"Me, too."

I assemble a cheese sandwich and add some baby carrots to the lunch bag—wishful thinking on my part, as Eliana is a vegetarian who doesn't like vegetables.

"It doesn't feel like home without Julia."

"I know."

She looks at her plate and pushes the eggs around with her fork.

"You okay, Sweetheart?"

She starts to cry. I kneel beside her chair and she lets me hug her. She doesn't like anyone to see her cry, so she hides her face in my chest till my shirt is damp. She wipes her nose on a striped pajama sleeve and looks up at me with red-rimmed eyes.

"Mom, when do I have surgery?"

"Next month. About six weeks."

"That's so soon!"

"I know."

Her mouth quivers, tears brimming again. She glances at the clock and shifts into high gear. "I can't be late for school!"

She bolts into her room, slams the door, emerges moments later in T-shirt and jeans, speed-braids her voluminous hair, tosses her homework and lunch bag in her backpack, and we're off.

I FALL INTO a daily routine, taking Eliana to school, walking through the labyrinthine paths of the Central Park Ramble, lying motionless on the radiation table. Those once excruciating sessions fly by, now that I've begun time-traveling with my mother. When Jamal says, in his beguiling Barbados accent, "Please lie perfectly still for ten minutes," it opens a portal through which I summon her. These telescoping minutes might last for days, or for just a few fleeting moments. We revisit events from our past together. Sometimes we just talk. Always, my mother is there and she is not there.

IN MY PERIPHERAL vision I see Mom leaning on the end of the radiation bed, ankles crossed, reading the *People* magazine I picked up in the waiting room. She's wearing a loose-fitting dress in an Indian paisley print, and she looks relaxed. It's comforting to have her in the room, watching over me.

"It's chilly in here. Are you cold, Sweetheart?" she asks.

"A little." The side of my face is pressed on the mattress. She pulls the sheet up and smooths it over my shoulders. "Thanks."

She goes back to reading the magazine. I listen to the pages flipping, and the customary electronic beeps and whirring of the machine.

"Mom, can I talk to you about something?"

"Of course."

"You never told me about your childhood."

"That's true." She puts the magazine down on the end of the bed.

"I learned about your Oklahoma roots years after you died. I always hated your secrets, and this was one more secret."

"I didn't intend for it to be a secret."

"Really? Well, it was, and it made me mad. You never told me a thing about your childhood or about Oklahoma! I talked to your brother, he told me to talk to your aunt, and I had to invent the rest. Makes me angry now, all over again. Why didn't you ever tell me?"

"You never asked."

"Okay. Sorry. I'm asking you now."

"Then I shall tell you now." She pushes her reading glasses up on top of her head and sits on the step stool next to my bed.

"I grew up in an unhappy home, in a big, dark house, in the orthodox Jewish neighborhood of Borough Park, Brooklyn. My family was affluent, relatively speaking. My father—your Grandpa Ben—was a well-respected doctor. His office was in the house, and we had to be very quiet when he was seeing patients. Our home was brimming with polished antique furniture, bookshelves laden with books and medical tomes and ivory bookends. Persian rugs, oil paintings, bronze figurines of Greek gods and goddesses, Tiffany lamps, silver tea sets, velvet drapes, and very little light."

As she talks, I picture her, simultaneously, as my fifty-seven-year-old mother and as a little girl in her dark house in Brooklyn.

"I lived with my mother, Rose, my father, Ben, my big brother, Edwin, and my horribly mean old Russian grandmother. Grandma spoke only Yiddish and hated my mother—her Oklahoma-born-and-bred, assimilated country hick of a Jewish daughter-in-law. I think my father loved Rose, but he was incapable of or unwilling to stand up to his toxic mother on his wife's behalf. My mother died in 1943, when I was twenty-two."

"That's how old I was when you died."

"Is that right? Yes, that's quite a coincidence. I used to visit Mother in the hospital after my classes at Columbia.

She had diabetes. She died from too much insulin and too little happiness."

"Please do not breathe so deeply, Ms. Cohen," says Jamal, over the speaker.

"Do you want me to continue?"

"Please."

"My father Ben grew up in Odessa. He studied to be a rabbi, before abandoning that career path to become a Marxist and a doctor. He spoke five languages, had a photographic memory, and liked to show off at every opportunity, by extemporaneously reciting entire pages of Shakespeare, Dostoyevsky, Gershwin, Puccini, and Tolstoy. When he quoted from *Anna Karenina*, 'All happy families are alike; each unhappy family is unhappy in its own way,' I was sure he was talking about us. Father didn't tolerate intellectual mediocrity, especially in his progeny. He disparaged my brother Edwin for his lack of ambition and set his sights on me, his high-achieving wunderkind daughter. He raised me with big words, great expectations, and enormous fear of his judgment.

"Every summer, my mother and my brother and I fled our claustrophobic home in Brooklyn for the wide expanses of Oklahoma. Our annual pilgrimage started with a two-day train-ride to Tulsa—and then on to the family homestead. We relished those summers on the peach farm with Grandpa Jake and Grandma Hattie. We hated having to go home. It was the only place my mother was truly happy. She was a farmer's daughter at heart. She was so alive there."

"Why'd you keep Oklahoma a secret, if it was so important to you?"

"I wanted to preserve the kernel of happiness Oklahoma represented, and feared it would be lost if I spoke about it out loud. Talking about it would be like opening Pandora's box. All hell breaks loose, and the potential for future happiness flies out. In social science terms, talking about Oklahoma was taboo. You see, what is considered taboo varies from culture to culture, depending on what commodity is in short supply: in a sexually repressed society, talking about sex is taboo; in a culture experiencing famine, it's taboo to talk about food—saying the word *yam* is the equivalent of telling a dirty joke, met with ribald laughter."

"So for you, *happiness* was the commodity in short supply. Thus, Oklahoma—representing *happiness*—was taboo."

"Exactly."

"Mom, you and I both lost our mothers twice: first to depression and then to death. Was it too painful for you to remember losing Rose? Is that why you exiled her from your memories?"

"Probably. Isn't that why you exiled me from yours?"

SCHOOL IS CLOSED for Yom Kippur. Madeline stays home with Eliana. I've rescheduled my radiation session for the afternoon so I can go to synagogue in the morning.

"On Rosh Hashanah it is written. On Yom Kippur it is sealed." We repeat this prayer throughout the day, chanting it in Hebrew and in English. On Rosh Hashanah, God inscribes the fate of every human being into the Book of Life—"*Who will live and who will die? Who shall be happy and who unhappy?*"—but God's judgment is not finalized until the book is closed, ten days later, on Yom Kippur.

Who gets happiness?

Was Aunt Phyllis able to love radiation because of her innate state of happiness? Does that explain her capacity to transform an "Oh Shit" moment into an "Aha!" moment? I think so. Her default barometer is set on feel-good. Even huge obstacles—and she's had some—don't derail her. They are simply temporary detours from her general state of contentment.

Is her propensity for happiness inherited? Learned? Willed?

Who gets to experience it all the time?

Who gets to experience it once in a while?

Who never gets it?

Where can I get some?

Is happiness a function of chemistry? Genetics? God?

If God, is it determined by God's mood, as God thumbs through the Book of Life, between Rosh Hashanah and Yom Kippur, deciding who shall live and who shall die? Does he also decide who shall be happy and who shall be sad or depressed or screwed up?

What is God thinking about, while marking up the Book of Life with editorial comments and directives in the margins? *"Live, die. Let's see . . . this one will break a toe; that one will get into her first-choice college; he will be hit by a bus and lose a leg; she will have one shorter leg.*

"You will get cancer and live happily for four more decades," like my mother's father, Ben.

"You will die depressed and sick at age forty-five," like my mother's mother, Rose.

"You will live happily to age a hundred and three," like Rose's little sister, Sylvia.

"You will be diagnosed with brain cancer at seventy-five and given only six months to live, but will survive another ten years," like my congenitally cheerful Uncle Edwin.

Edwin was more resilient than my mother was. The jovial, self-proclaimed absent-minded professor, renowned for his Brooklyn College courses on Moral Development, Ed's contentment was irrepressible and infectious. Whatever my mother's mood, she would always brighten up in her brother's presence. When we visited Uncle Ed, the moment we walked through the door he would launch into song—an operatic recitative about whatever happened to be on his mind—improvised in loosely rhymed verses:

Welcome, my darling sister, Louise!
Take off your coat. Have a drink. Sit down, please.
Come in, come right in, my three lovely nieces!
May I interest you girls in some nice, stinky cheeses?

Then Mom would sing with him. Just *because*. It was silly and entertaining, and we understood that she *only* did this with her brother:

It's a pleasure, dear Ed, to drink sherry with you,
But first, I've a question, or maybe a few.
What books are you reading? What conceptual forces
Are driving your Moral Development courses?

Uncle Ed would pull a book from his vast bookshelves, open to a page, and paraphrase—in song:

(To the tune of "The Hallelujah Chorus")
Mar-tin Buber!
Mar-tin Buber!
"I and Thou!"—Not
"I and It!"—That's
—his Phi-*lo*-so-*phy*!

Then, Uncle Edwin would pick up his violin and play some scratchy melodies, while my Aunt Abby served the sherry and stinky cheeses.

When Edwin was diagnosed with brain cancer, his right jaw and skull were surgically carved away, bit by bit, year after year, until he looked like he was wearing an expressionistic mask, his mouth a diagonal line on the far right side of his decimated face. Even so, he woke up every morning beside his beloved wife of sixty years, happy to be on earth another day, joking, "What do you know, Abby-girl? I'm still alive!"

"You, Alice, will be the brooding sister."

"You, Julia, will inherit your birth mother's lightness of spirit."

"You, Eliana, will inherit your mother's propensity for brooding."

Are the infinite varieties of the human condition randomly assigned? God's capricious whims? Or a meditative, thoughtful, and painful endeavor? Like making art. Is God plotting the beats in our collective lives with parental compassion? Or is it a creative act? Is she writing fiction, inventing characters for an epic novel? Is he the head writer for an ongoing soap opera called *Life on Earth*?

I try to achieve an Aunt Phyllis–like state of euphoria during treatments. There are times when I approach it, lying nearly motionless on the radiation table, when my shallow breathing slows, and the itch on my nose that's been driving me crazy fades from consciousness.

At those moments, like right now, lying facedown in a room as sterile as a space capsule, I enter a Zen state of equilibrium, akin to happiness. But unlike Aunt Phyllis, I have to consciously will it, and must work hard to maintain it.

I carefully set my compass on a course headed toward joy, fretfully checking to see that I haven't veered off course, that I'm not sailing straight back to the black hole of sadness where I've already spent too much time. Like my mother did, and her mother, too.

THREE

"We were close, weren't we, Mom? Before your cancer?"

"Yes. That was a dreadful turning point. It wasn't the end, but that was our great divide. There was a before and an after."

"The after was when all hell broke loose."

"For both of us."

I was twelve. Tomorrow, I would start eighth grade. I looked at myself in the mirror, previewed my back-to-school outfit—red miniskirt, black turtleneck, black fishnet tights. I stuck my skinny chest out, trying to look like an eighth grader, but I still looked like a little girl.

On the last day of seventh grade, Dad took Mom to the hospital. He didn't tell us why. When she was away for three days, I was sure she had died.

Then Mom's best friend Shirley called.

"Hello, Alice, dear. I'm so sorry about your mom. Tell me, darling, did she have one breast removed or two?"

I didn't understand Shirley's question. I couldn't imagine why breasts would be removed.

". . . Alice? Are you there? One or both?"

"Um. Um. One. I think just one."

"Well, that's a relief, isn't it? At least it was only one."

I was wrong.

Once Mom came back from the hospital she was changed. No longer the mother I knew. No longer the mother who smiled and laughed and grew flowers and napped on the hammock so the birds would land on her. No longer the mother who once loved me so much, the mother who hugged me, called me Sweetheart and Honey-lamb and Sweetiepie, who said she loved me to pieces, who praised my drawings, who did "X Marks the Spot" on my back, over and over, as many times as I asked. This other mother barely noticed us. She was an imposter. Like the Mean Mother from the bad dream I used to have. My mom didn't actually die, but she was gone.

Dad didn't talk to us very much all summer. He came home from work and played piano for hours. Chopin. Beethoven. Mozart. Brahms. Gershwin. Bach. Sometimes he and I played clarinet-piano duets together. I was getting good at clarinet. We were practicing the Brahms sonatas.

I looked in the mirror again. I was the youngest in my grade and I was completely flat. This was going to be so embarrassing. I'd be the last girl still wearing an undershirt. Maybe, maybe, maybe Mom would take me shopping for a training bra, like all the other mothers of every girl I knew. I hoped she would.

No. This wasn't the time to ask my mother to take me bra shopping.

In the schoolyard, some of the fourth graders are flirting with each other. Their juvenile attempts are bumbling, graceless, and adorable. The boys intentionally bump into the girls. The girls push the boys and run away laughing. And so it begins. Eliana isn't yet interested in boys in that way, which is fine with me. The only boy she considers a close friend is James, her best friend since they were three years old.

I was fourteen. It was August 1969, two years after Mom's surgery. I was home from a month at music camp, where

I played in an orchestra for the first time; where I got drunk for the first time; where, unbeknownst to me, another camper slipped acid into my hive medicine and I unwittingly tripped for the first time (and *last* time—what a nightmare!); and where I suddenly, unintentionally, flamboyantly, extravagantly, conspicuously reached puberty. My breasts grew so fast, you could watch their size increase with every passing day; for the boys, it was a spectator sport.

I came home with my brand-new breasts, and there was Mom with none at all.

"Falsies" is an embarrassing word.

Everything is embarrassing when you're fourteen.

Nothing is more embarrassing than your mother's falsies.

Mom wore a crude prosthetic, a padded bra, which slid around, telegraphing to the world that she had "falsies."

It was like she hated that I was suddenly sexual, and she was suddenly not.

At music camp, my new figure made me a catch to the predatory boys. Squirrel to their falcon. A minute ago, I was a little girl, and—*Boom!*—now I was a sexpot. Ogled, pursued, invited to join illicit midnight skinny-dippings in the pool. It was dangerous, fun, titillating. And it was too much, it was overwhelming, confusing.

I was having a secret romance with David, the eighteen-year-old counselor who taught woodwinds and conducted the chamber music ensemble. The first week, we took secret walks in the woods, holding hands. One afternoon, he pulled away from me, stared at me with a crazed look, and abruptly unzipped his jeans and ripped them off.

I was thinking, "Oh my God, oh my God, this is it! David is overcome with sexual desire. He's taking his pants off. What's going to happen next? Am I ready for this?"

There was a praying mantis crawling up David's thigh. A six-inch twig with legs. He flicked it off, and I laughed my head off. He laughed, too, then pulled his jeans back on.

That night in my cabin, according to plan, I tied a long piece of string around my wrist, and threaded it through the knothole in the wall beside my top bunk. David tugged on the string to wake me at midnight—very Romeo and Juliet—and I quietly climbed down from my bunk, tiptoed past Sheila the counselor, and out of the cabin. We ran into the pine forest and snuck into an abandoned cabin David had the key to. We took our clothes off. I learned about male anatomy, a new subject for me. There was lots of touching and stroking and fon-dling, no more than that, but it was a lot. I still felt like a little kid, wearing the strangely persuasive costume of a young woman.

We were busted in the middle of the night, naked in the cabin in the woods. Flashlights on us. David was fired. The camp director called my parents.

Mom was furious.

With camp? With David? With me?

Yes and yes and yes.

When I went home at the end of the summer, buxom and fattened up from camp food so bad that all the kids filled up instead on white bread slathered with butter and sugar, my mother looked at me like she didn't rec-ognize me.

She looked at me with . . . what is it? Disgust? Envy? Fury? Loss?

Yes and yes and yes and yes.

Mom forbade me from ever seeing David again.

"He's too old for you, Alice. You're in tenth grade. What is a college freshman doing with a fourteen-year-old?"

"Almost fifteen!"

"I don't trust him."

"You haven't met him!"

"I don't want to meet him."

I ran to the living room where Dad was at the piano, playing Chopin.

Mom followed me, arms crossed, lips pursed.

Dad finished playing, then turned to face me.

"What's wrong, Alice?"

"Please let me see David. We're in love!"

Jennifer, my goofy-looking little sister, looked up from her book, eyes wide, her crooked teeth facing every which way.

"You know me," said Dad, chuckling, turning it into a joke, "I don't know a damn thing about relationships. All I understand is music, and since David is a classically trained musician, in my book, he's—"

"Ira!" snapped Mom.

"Uh . . . Listen to your mother, Alice."

"Daddy, please!"

"Your mother says no. So that's that."

"This is so unfair!" I ran upstairs to my room and threw myself on the bed, sobbing, Juliet separated from her Romeo. Amanda the Cat jumped on my bed, licked my face and purred. She always did that when I cried. I wanted to believe it was affection, but I think she just liked the salt. I took out my stash of love letters from David—he wrote me long, flowery, idolatrous letters every day—and I cried some more.

MY SISTER MADELINE was going back to college. We drove up to Boston and helped her move into her new dorm room at Brandeis. Gone, just when we needed her the most. Madeline didn't live with us anymore. Jennifer and I were sad that she wasn't home. Why did she have to leave now? Madeline always saw the bright side of things. With Mom angry all the time, we could have used Madeline's calming infuence.

Mom was always glaring at me. Sometimes she stood behind me and insulted me, while I was looking in the mirror. She had never insulted me before. Never said stuff like this to me, never before this summer. She was acting crazy. I got the feeling she couldn't say this stuff to my face because she knew it was wrong.

"You're getting fat," she told my reflection.

"Leave me alone."

"Your legs look like stuffed sausages."

"Leave me alone!"

"Your breasts are enormous."

I started to cry. "Stop it!" I put my hands over my ears.

"You eat too much. Have a yogurt for dinner, *or* a bowl of soup."

"Shut! Up!"

"Not both. I'm concerned about your health. You used to be—"

"Don't!"

"—so slender and pretty, and—"

"Please leave me alone!"

"Now look at you!"

"Get out of my room, Mom!"

"Are you pregnant?"

"GET OUT!"

DAVID WENT TO college in Boston. He wrote me long love letters and took the train every weekend to see me. We would meet up secretly at the home of his friend Ralph, a senior at my high school, who had also met David at music camp. David recently had a falling out with his parents, and they locked him out of their New York City apartment where David grew up, so David would crash at Ralph's on the weekends. But now, even Ralph's laid-back parents were tiring of David, who had a habit of getting kicked out of places. The two guys cooked up elaborate schemes for our clandestine meetings, which once entailed my climbing into Ralph's second-floor bedroom window via the maple tree in his backyard.

Sometimes, David brazenly knocked on my front door. If Mom was out and Dad was home, I would let him in, and they'd talk about music. He successfully wooed my father with his musical passions: they had the same favorite conductor (Bernstein), same favorite orchestra (Philadelphia), same favorite composer (Beethoven). He made my dad positively ecstatic by playing duets with him.

But as soon as my mother came home, the music stopped.

"Get out of my house."

"With all due respect, Mrs. Cohen—"

"Shut up!"

It was sort of a relief when David and Mom fought over me. I was momentarily out of the spotlight. Dad ignored them and played piano, providing the soundtrack to their arguments. Jennifer and I sat on the sofa, observing Mom and David's back and forth debate, as if we were watching a tennis match. Jennifer worshipped me and my teenaged friends. In Jennifer's eyes, I could do no wrong.

David sometimes went to outrageous lengths to try to win over my mom.

"Mrs. Cohen, I noticed that your floors needed mopping and waxing, so while you were out, I took it upon myself to . . ."

The floor shone under its slippery coat of wax. My mother was momentarily speechless, stupefied by the deafening clash of gratitude and rage.

"It was very nice of you to mop the floor, David. Thank you, but it doesn't change my opinion. Now leave."

"Mrs. Cohen, with all due respect, I know you don't trust me—"

"You're right, I don't."

"But I want you to know that Alice and I are not having sex."

"I should hope not!"

Technically speaking, David and I were not having sex. We did other things, but we'd never had intercourse. Mom probably assumed we had, but I was so mad at her, I wouldn't admit to her that I was a virgin.

"Alice," Mom scowled at me in the mirror, "I looked through your sketchbook—"

"Don't look at my sketchbook!"

"—and I saw your drawings of naked couples having sex."

"That's private!"

"Are you having sex?

"They're just drawings! Stay out of my stuff."

She sighed, stared at me for a full minute, with who knows what thoughts going through her mind, then said, "You're drawings . . . are excellent."

DAD AND I didn't talk much. It wasn't his style. Cheerful detachment was his style. He avoided emotional confrontation by keeping himself busy: doing calisthenics every morning when he woke up, working in his office all day, playing piano every night, sailing every weekend. My parents argued about sailing. Mom thought he should spend less time sailing and more time with his family. He was stubborn about doing what he wanted to do, when he wanted to do it. I wasn't good at sailing. Neither was Mom or my sisters, so Dad was off limits on weekends when he raced with his expert crew.

The way to reach Dad was through music. He took me to my clarinet lesson every Thursday evening. We played clarinet-piano sonatas together. It made us both happy. It was the only way I knew how to feel close to him, to get his attention. My playing impressed Grandpa Ben, who proclaimed in his thick Russian accent that I was destined for a world-class concert career (though his considerable hearing loss cast doubt on his assessment of my talent.) The only one in the family who didn't like my clarinet playing was Amanda. As soon as I started playing, she flattened her ears, ran to the door, scratched on the screen, and meowed pitifully, begging to be let out.

Music was a reliable way to escape my mother's weird anger at me. She didn't yell at me or insult me when I was practicing, so I practiced a lot.

When I was a little girl, I once threw a block at Sally and chipped her tooth for saying my mom was crazy, but now I wondered whether it was true. My mom was so different from other moms. Over the summer, while I was at camp, Mom gave up stockings. She gave up high heels. She gave up lipstick. She gave up shaving her legs. She gave up dyeing her hair. She gave up acting like other middle-aged suburban moms. She didn't look or behave like any of the other moms I knew.

She was a mad woman. Not a madwoman. She was a woman who was mad all the time. She was mostly mad at the trappings of being a suburban wife, so she had jettisoned them, one by one. What would she give up next? From the way she was looking at me, I thought she wanted to give up being my mother.

At the end of tenth grade, I broke up with David. It was my decision. "I can't stand having my mother angry with me all the time," I told him after that awful year. "It makes me miserable. And I'm not in love with you anymore."

But even with David out of the picture, Mom still seemed to be angry with me.

When I pick up Eliana from school, she and her classmate Thomas are intentionally bumping into each other, shoulder to shoulder, in that fourth-grade way that could be aggression or flirtation, or an amalgam of both. I picture Eliana a few years from now, as a fourteen-year-old. Oh, my God, I would hate it if either of my daughters at age fourteen had a love affair with a college student. I would forbid it. I'd be furious. What was I thinking? Of course David was too old for me. Of course my mother was right.

Pelting rain. The motor was idling. The windshield wipers swished back and forth, to no purpose. I sat in the passenger seat next to Mom, my face in my hands, hoping none of my classmates would see me through the wall of water. Students huddled under umbrellas and ponchos near the high-school entrance. The bell rang, and they shoved through the glass doors.

"Mom. Please don't go into school like that."

"Why not?" she snapped.

"Because you're wearing a nightgown!"

"I have a raincoat over it. Nobody will notice."

"Yes they will! Everyone will notice."

"Who cares what I'm wearing?"

"I do!"

"Well, I don't. I'm angry, and I need to have a word with the principal. If I phone he'll ignore me. I can get his attention if I go into school now."

"Yeah, you'll get his attention alright!"

She turned off the engine. "Are you coming?"

"Don't go into school like that."

"Are you coming or not, Alice?"

"No," I groaned. "I'll wait till you're inside."

"Fine!" she seethed. She turned off the engine, got out of the car, and slammed the door behind her. I watched her run through the pouring rain in her slippers, her long white nightgown dragging in the puddles.

My mother was usually angry *at* me. But today she was angry *for* me, which was even worse. She periodically marched into the high school office in her nightgown to complain about some meaningless bullshit—my intense homework load, or my heavy backpack, or some other idiotic notion that she had blown way out of proportion. I was mortified by her public displays.

The late bell rang. I waited in the car till she was out of sight before slinking soggily into school. Later, through the open door of my first-period Spanish class, I saw the assistant principal escort my mother out of his office and into the hall, where he jutted his chin out and called her an "irate parent" in his gruff, retired-army-sergeant voice, before letting go of her elbow. There was giggling in the classroom. My cheeks burned. I stared hard at my notebook and scribbled hieroglyphics in the margins. Some of my classmates were staring at my mother, the lady in the nightgown and trench coat. Some were staring at me.

"¡Atención, clase! Escúchame, y repita lo que digo," said Señora Delgado, tactfully and mercifully closing the door.

Every morning, after walking Eliana to school, I take a different path through Central Park. This is my favorite part of the day. Purple morning glories line the fence around Sheep's Meadow. Turtles line up on the boulders bordering the lake. Bright yellow leaves carpet the trails near the Boathouse. Jugglers and musicians practice at the Bethesda Fountain. In a hidden pond, I see orange carp, pond skimmers, emerald dragonflies. There's an aerial party around the birdfeeders, a cacophonous symphony of birdsong. I walk on soft grass and dirt paths, and scramble to the top of boulders, pretending that I'm on the Appalachian Trail, rather than in the middle of Manhattan.

Signs at trailheads designate the Ramble FOREVER WILD—albeit a loose definition of *wild*. Central Park is a carefully landscaped illusion of nature, designed in 1858 by Frederick Law Olmstead, maintained these days by the Central Park Conservancy. The purported "wild" parts are fenced in. Obedient tourists and locals stay on the paved paths. A man-made waterfall flows into the man-made lake. I'm sure the multi-ton boulders were deposited here by retreating glaciers in the last Ice Age, but what about that huge gray slab of stone, artfully silhouetted against the lake? Was that the work of Mother Nature or Mr. Olmstead?

I'm amused by the trompe l'oeil effect. I like being tricked into thinking I'm in nature, when this park is as carefully contrived as Disneyland. Anyway, the trees don't give a damn that they were planted by a landscape designer. The ducks don't care that the lake is a ruse, fed by an underground plumbing system. To the thousands of migratory birds that land in Central Park each spring and fall, Central Park is an oasis of forest and ponds, not an elaborate stage set. They have no argument with the human landscaping, or with humans for that matter. I figure, if birds are tricked by Central Park, there's no shame in being tricked myself.

It was 1971, and I was sixteen. Eleventh grade.

One day, Mom abandoned the falsies and went natural. Very Women's Lib, except that the all-natural, braless attitude was more of an under-thirty thing, and braless feminists generally had breasts. But this was very Mom. Breastless and restless. She was already the only woman in our constrictive suburban ecosystem to *not* mow the lawn to precisely match the tacitly approved crew cut of the neighbors' lawns. She was the only woman in our neighborhood who went to antiwar protests, who held two master's degrees from Columbia University (Sociology, and Public Law and Government), who had contributed as a researcher to two books developed by renowned anthropologist Margaret Mead, and who was working on a monumental, ever-growing, ever-unfinished, PhD dissertation.

Mom had attained an enlightened state of antivanity. I admired her nonconformity, I really did. I was grateful that we went on family trips to antiwar marches on Washington. That was cool. I was glad she was a feminist. I should have been proud of her, but she embarrassed me. Her tirades at my school had made her the brunt of jokes. "Alice's mother is weird, she's crazy," my classmates whispered. I wanted to punch them in the face, but I just walked past them, my cheeks burning.

MEANWHILE, MOM STILL acted like she hated me.
"I don't want to be called Mommy ever again."
"Should I call you Mom?
"That's just as bad."
"Okay, you want me to call you Louise?"
"That's better."
She used to love me. What did I do? Grow up? Reach puberty? Nothing I could do about it. She never used to say mean things to me. I wanted to cry, but I was sixteen, so what could I do except be angry back at her? I was so angry I ate a whole box of Fig Newtons. That would show her. Ha!

Some days I hated *her.* I never used to. It was because of her stupid breast cancer. It ruined everything.

But I didn't really hate her. I missed her. She probably didn't really hate me, either. She liked my good grades and my artwork. I won an art contest in *Seventeen* magazine, and she showed everyone the issue with my prize-winning collage published in it! She probably missed me. She probably missed herself. Why did she have to get breast cancer? I hated, hated, hated cancer.

She hated my boyfriend, Paul—more than was logically possible. I thought she also liked him, but she wouldn't admit it. How could she not have liked him? He was fantastic. I was totally in love with him. We met at All-County Choir. Paul was in a band, and he played guitar and sang exactly like James Taylor. He was a year older than me and he lived two towns over. We biked six miles to visit each other. He was super smart and super nice, tall and lanky, gorgeous, sexy, and oh my God, what an amazing kisser. We only made out, which was fine with me—lovely, actually. We were crazy about each other. I was so happy we were together. Paul had drawn a scarily low number in the draft lottery, but he got into Cornell, so he'd be safe for the next four years. His mother, Beverly, said if he was drafted they'd move to Canada. Beverly was cool. She liked me a lot, which was nice but kind of surreal, in light of my mother's low regard for her son. She was a teacher, really smart and interesting, very liberal. In fact, she reminded me a lot of *my* mother before she became angry all the time.

The more Mom hated Paul, the more I loved him. She unwittingly regulated our mother–daughter emotional thermostat. The more she dialed up the heat on her anger, the more my passion for Paul increased, till I was on fire. Dial it on up, Mom! She was probably jealous.

Mom and Dad barely ever touched. Did that mean they never had sex? (I didn't want to think about that.)

Then Paul went to Cornell. We continued our romance long-distance, until he started dating Caroline. The morning Mom figured it out (my bloodshot eyes gave me away), she launched into a ferocious monologue at the breakfast table, while brutally slicing a loaf of bread.

"Paul is despicable, unfaithful, false-hearted . . ."

I begged her to stop. I was still in love with Paul and I couldn't stand hearing her rail against him, but she was unstoppable. She continued to assault the bread, while spewing a thesaurus-worthy litany of invective.

"He's deceitful, duplicitous, perfidious, hateful . . ."

"Shut up!" I yelled, covering my ears, but Mom was just revving up.

Jennifer ate her frosted flakes, silent and attentive, her silver braces gleaming.

". . . fickle, treacherous, cheating . . ."

Her anger was way out of proportion. I was the one who should be angry, not her. But now I couldn't be angry at Paul, because Mom had stolen my anger.

". . . underhanded, lying . . ."

I had to defend Paul's honor, even though he'd just broken up with me. I wanted to kill Mom, Mommy, Mother, Louise, whatever the fuck she wanted me to call her today. I wanted to stab her with the bread knife. I actually wanted to do that. I pictured myself grabbing the knife and stabbing her in the chest.

This was such a horrifying thought that I ran to my room and threw myself on my bed, sobbing. I ignored Mom when she knocked on my door. I ignored her ten minutes later, when she offered to drive me to school. I put my *Sweet Baby James* album on at full volume to drown her out.

After she left with Jennifer, I walked to school, arriving very late. My red, puffy eyes sufficed as explanation and excuse—the universal alibi of female adolescent angst. The teacher didn't even mark me late.

That night there was a typed letter on my pillow.

Dear Alice—I regret that I was so bitter and caused you so much anguish this morning. It is not you—but Paul—who

angers me. However, I truly do not understand and may
therefore be misinterpreting and distorting the situation. But
I would rather be of help—than a source of grief . . . Mother

I'm sure she meant it, but she failed. I didn't understand her. "I regret that I was so bitter and caused you
so much anguish." Yeah, I regretted that, too. What was
wrong with her? I was the jilted one, but I got it. Paul
went to college and his feelings changed. Out of sight, out
of mind. I hated it, but I got it. Stuff like that happened;
everybody knew that. She didn't make sense. I couldn't
trust her. She *was* a source of grief, whether or not she
intended to be. No, I didn't think she could help me. I
didn't want her help.

"When my leg is lengthened, won't my shoe lift be too
big?" Eliana asks on our way to the shoe store.

"Good point."

"Won't we have to make the lift shorter and shorter
while my leg is getting longer and longer?"

"I think you're right."

Buying shoes for Eliana is a challenge. We can't buy
her any old cheap shoes. They have to be high-quality,
supportive shoes, made from a material that Herman the

Shoe Lift Guy can work with. Herman will cut off a thin layer from the bottom of the sole and sandwich a customized three-inch lift between the shoe and the bottom of the sole. To further complicate matters, Eliana's right foot is two sizes smaller than her left. For every pair of shoes she wears, I have to buy two pairs, in two different sizes. Her right foot fits into little kid sizes, and her left foot fits into big-kid sizes. Few shoe styles are made for both little and big kids, so our choices are limited. And expensive. At $50 a pair x 2 pairs + $130 for the shoe lift, each pair of shoes Eliana wears costs $230.

She chooses blue Nikes, red Nikes, and black Mary Janes, for which I purchase six pairs of shoes. Of the twelve new shoes we carry out of the store, six will never be worn. I'll bring the three smaller-size right shoes to Herman after radiation tomorrow. His shop is a block from NYU Cancer Center, near *da corner of Toidy-toid and Toid*.

I still climbed the tree in our yard now and then (even though twelfth grade was considered too old to climb trees), to have some privacy, some peace and quiet; and to spy on the neighborhood. One day, I saw the Ramirez kids, Miguel and Rosalia, go in our side door and come out with an armload of food. I didn't say anything.

Another day, from the tree, I saw Dad and Mom arguing in the kitchen. I couldn't hear what they were saying,
but I could tell that Dad was trying to make light of the
argument, as was his habit. He flashed a charming smile
at Mom, but his charm wasn't working today. He tried to
hug her, but she pulled away. He looked hurt. He opened
his arms to her and made a sweet, imploring face. She
wiped tears away. He tried again to hug her. She pushed
him away. Her eyes shot daggers at him. She shouted
something. She was an irate wife. He hung his head and
put his hands in his pockets.

Why was she so angry? What were they saying? It was
like watching a silent movie. I imagined the captions to
the melodrama playing out in the kitchen.

> "You don't love me anymore."
> "Of course I do!"
> "No you don't. Not since my operation."
> "Louise—"
> "Don't lie to me."

Was there another woman? Dad with someone else?
That would be weird. I was just guessing, playing detec-
tive. I didn't know and I didn't want to know. Maybe she
was just angry at him for sailing every weekend and never

being home. Whatever the cause, I surmised that she was angry with him and taking it out on me. Her crazy, intense anger at Paul leaving me for another girl was her misplaced anger at Dad. Maybe. I should have been glad that she was arguing with Dad, so she would cut me some slack. No, of course I wasn't glad that they were fighting. It made me sad. And mad. At Dad—I mean, if he was having an affair, and I didn't know if he was.

Herman flashes his irresistible smile at me, as he walks slowly from the back of the store, carefully shifting his weight to accommodate his prosthetic leg. He's in his forties, but his broad face is boyish and cherubic. He lost his leg at age six, when he was hit by a bus in his native Colombia. I think he's heroic for choosing a career that allows him to help other people to walk. He makes brilliant shoe lifts for Eliana. No one is better than Herman.

"How ya doin'," he says, giving me a hug and a kiss on the cheek. He grabs a stool and sits across from me to study Eliana's new shoes. He wears his customary white canvas work apron over a plaid button-down shirt, neat blue jeans, and running shoes.

"How's my baby? You bring pictures?"

I hand him a photo of Eliana at camp, walking Alex the Llama.

"She's getting so big! This one's goin' on my Wall of Fame."

Herman's Wall of Fame has photos, letters, and artifacts from his favorite customers, including a seven-foot-tall teenager from Illinois, for whom Herman makes size 20 sneakers; a little boy with a degenerative skin disease, for whom Herman creates soft, nonchafing shoes; a Barnum & Bailey Circus clown with bunions, for whom Herman makes customized clown shoes; and Eliana.

"I want to see pictures, too," I say, and Herman produces snapshots of the foster babies he and his wife are caring for. I love this guy, for helping my kid and all these other kids, for being incredibly kind.

"What are we doin' today?"

"Three shoe lifts. Next month, Eliana has that leg-lengthening surgery I told you about."

"We'll have to make the lifts shorter while her leg is getting longer."

"That's just what Eliana said."

"Smart girl! That's my baby. I'll call you when these are ready."

• • •

I saw a wild turkey in the Ramble today. It was strolling on a patch of sundrenched grass where a group of orthodox Jewish preschoolers was playing kickball. I've never seen a turkey in the park before. He looked conspicuously out of place, big, ungainly, and vulnerable. I didn't know there were wild turkeys in the park. I asked a park ranger, who said the turkey flew into the park a week ago, and all the rangers are worried about him because he's alone and will never find a mate unless he flies away.

Julia hasn't responded to my assorted phone calls and e-mails. I finally snag her attention with a jokey e-mail subject, *"JULIA, CALL NOW TO COLLECT YOUR PRIZE MONEY!"* I happen to be at my computer when her e-mail comes in at one in the morning.

"Everything's fine, Mom. Sorry I haven't called. Princeton's great. I miss you too, and yes, I'm coming home for fall break. Can't wait to sleep in my own bed. But I won't be home the whole week, just 2 days. Have to be back Oct 30 for crew practice. I made VARSITY! Can you believe it? Hardly any freshman walk-ons made the cut. Who knew I'd ever be an athlete?"

I grab the phone and call her.

"Hey, Mom, what are you doing up so late?"

"Waiting for your e-mail. Just kidding. What are *you* doing up so late?"

She laughs. "This isn't late for me."

"I knew that."

"I have a paper due tomorrow."

Lady Gaga's "Poker Face" plays in the background. I hear her roommate singing along. I picture Julia in her plaid flannel pajamas, sitting cross-legged on the narrow bed in her cozy dorm room, typing her paper, answering e-mails, listening to music, singing with her roommate, talking to me. She's expert at multitasking.

"I miss you, Julia. It's good to hear your voice."

"You, too."

"I should go to sleep."

"I have miles to go before I sleep."

Three weeks before I started college, we moved to a house on the other side of town, in Shore Acres, near the beach. My parents sold our old house on Wilbur Avenue to Charles Raymond, a well-known businessman in town. Charles owned The Record Shop, where Madeline had an after-school job in 1967, selling Joni Mitchell,

Rolling Stones, Richie Havens, Simon and Garfunkel, and Joan Baez albums. He was the first black person to live in my old neighborhood. And the first mixed-race family—Charles's wife was Swedish. Their two young, beautiful children had light brown skin and kinky, golden hair.

There was ugly racial hostility toward the Raymonds in our blue-collar neighborhood. I heard through the grapevine that the neighbors had circulated a petition to keep them out.

The banks had rejected the Raymonds' loan application, even though Charles was a long-established local businessman. When my parents guaranteed the loan, the banks had no more excuse to reject him.

I was proud of my parents for helping Charles, especially after my mother's years of civil rights campaigning in our narrow-minded neighborhood. But I was worried about their kids—if the neighbors dumped garbage in our yard and slashed our bike tires for being Jewish, what indignities would they concoct for the Raymonds? On the other hand, the Raymonds kept their lawn tidily mowed.

I was surprised that my parents could afford to move to Shore Acres. I was having an identity crisis. What social class did we belong to, now that my parents were moving to a more affluent neighborhood, with other Jewish families around? I felt betrayed, and like a betrayer. Fitting in here made me feel alienated in a brand-new way. It was a simple ranch house, nothing fancy, but I had to admit it was nice to be able to walk to the beach, from an address that gave us beach privileges. (It was a guilty pleasure: I remembered Mom leading us on a low-tide trek across the beach in Martha's Vineyard, to fight for public waterfront access.)

Mom wasn't so angry anymore. She was happy about moving. And I think she was happy about me leaving home, even though we weren't fighting now—a tentative truce. She said she was proud of me.

"You'll love college, I just know it. Keep making art. Study what you're passionate about, that's paramount," she told me at breakfast in the new dining room (our old house didn't have a dining room), with a picture window overlooking a gently sloping, neatly mowed lawn.

"But don't forget that you'll need to make a living when you graduate," added my dad, enthusiastically slicing strawberries and peaches on his cornflakes and digging in with gusto.

My parents were still tense with each other. But Mom

looked healthier, and she liked her new job, leading a seminar for nurses at Columbia Presbyterian Hospital.

"The nurses in my seminar are angry and frustrated because they have no power," she told me, Jennifer, and Dad as she served dinner. While she continued her lecture, we feasted on peak-season corn on the cob, juicy beefsteak tomatoes, and velvety bib lettuce that Mom had bought at the local farm stand—she had an uncanny ability to choose perfect fruits and vegetables. "Doctors give their nurses huge responsibilities, but no respect. When a doctor makes a mistake, the nurse is often the one who saves the patient's life, but doctors resent the nurses who correct them. They're either ignored or punished for insubordination. And of course there's the disparity in pay. All these unwritten covenants of discrimination, the conspiracy of silent acceptance. The exciting thing is that, finally, these nurses aren't accepting the silence anymore. They insist on being heard."

After dinner, Jennifer and I cleaned up, Dad practiced a Beethoven piano sonata, and Mom went into her study. She had the same old-fashioned typewriter, but she no longer had to type at the kitchen table. She finally had a room of her own.

When the dishes were done, I quietly entered Mom's

study, a serene room overlooking a tidal marsh, habitat to a large variety of birds, which of course she loved. Redwing blackbirds flitted between cattails, a white egret moved in slow motion toward its prey, a great blue heron soared over the tall reeds, showing off his impressive wingspan.

She was still working on her sociology dissertation for Columbia University, trying to get her PhD so she could advance from her low-paid, underappreciated adjunct professor status: she was teaching a smattering of courses at City University, Pace College, and Columbia Teachers College, as well as the nursing seminar. I surmised that the nurses might be the topic of her doctoral dissertation. She typed and typed, tearing out pages, sorting them into mountains—rough drafts, edited drafts, carbon copies, rejects. Now that she had her own desk, she could spread out and make a mess. The precarious mountains of paper resembled volcanoes, loose pages cascading like lava down the slopes. Her fingers flew over the keys, trying to keep up with her ideas, but her ideas came faster. Her right hand reflexively hit the return at the end of every line, then pulled the finished page from the typewriter with a ratcheting sound.

"Mom—"

"Yes, Alice?"

"I'm . . . I think I'm going to miss you. When I'm at college."

She stopped typing and looked at me, surprised, as if she had just heard the word *college* for the first time, as if my going to college were an entirely new concept. "I think I'm going to miss you, too, Sweetheart."

FOUR

Flipping through magazines in the waiting room, I come across an article about the increased risk of breast cancer for women who took Hormone Replacement Therapy. *Blah!* I was on HRT for fourteen years. And that's just the latest chapter of my epic hormonal odyssey. I could write a book. My life, seen through estrogen-colored glasses:

PHARMACEUTICAL PHRANKENSTEIN
MONSTER MASHUP
A memoir
by Alice Eve Cohen

Chapter 1: ITSY BITSY BABY (PART ONE)
Once upon a time, long, long ago (c. 1954), when I was but a wee little zygote, I was exposed to DES,

the antimiscarriage drug my mother took when she became pregnant with me, after three miscarriages.

In the baby-booming fifties, the synthetic estrogen DES (diethylstibestrol) was routinely prescribed by doctors as the "pregnancy vitamin," the silver bullet that would prevent miscarriage and ensure healthy, booming babies. Eli Lilly and the other drug companies soon discovered that DES was: (1) completely ineffective in preventing miscarriage, *and* (2) carcinogenic. But they hid the damning evidence and continued to promote the drug for two more decades, while DES wreaked havoc, causing birth defects, cancers in the reproductive organs, infertility, and increased risk of breast cancer—both in the mothers who took the drug (Exhibit A: Mom) and in their daughters (Exhibit B: me).

CHAPTER 2: BABY BOOMER ACTIVIST

When I was thirty, I joined a class-action lawsuit, which collectively attempted to sue Eli Lilly's ass (Lilly only experienced a small pinch.) I collected a small out-of-court settlement for my infertility. I wrote a play about DES. My cervix became world-famous—videotaped for medical students, because my weird cells illustrated the classic DES abnormalities.

CHAPTER 3: THE INFERTILE ERA

From age thirty to forty-four, I was prescribed HRT to treat low estrogen, which, as it turned out, I didn't need. (Exhibit C: my unexpected pregnancy with Eliana, fourteen years after being told that my estrogen was so low I could never, ever, ever, *ever*, EVER become pregnant.)

CHAPTER 4: ITSY BITSY BABY (PART TWO)

Once upon a time, long, long ago (c. 1999), when Eliana was but a wee zygote, she was exposed to the synthetic hormones I was taking, and continued to take for the first two trimesters.

Does this sound familiar?

Is this some kind of a family curse? Family legacy? Family joke?

Life-long exposure to synthetic hormones may have caused my breast cancer.

My mother's breast cancer may have been caused by DES.

These strange symmetries lead to strange asymmetries.

When my radiation treatment is over, I'll take an estrogen-blocker for five years, which is ironic, if not funny, if not *hysterical*—from the Greek, *hustera,* which means "womb," which is etymologically ironic.

After a lifetime of being pumped with estrogen drugs, my natural estrogen is going to be *blocked* for the next five years with yet another synthetic estrogen. I am a magnet for medical ironies.

This makes me really mad. If I get any madder, I'll become a *madwoman.* I might become completely *hysterical.* I bet I'm the only woman in history *(hystery)* to have sued for both infertility and fertility.

OH, GOD, HOW I wish I hadn't inadvertently drugged and dragged Eliana into this, before she was born.

Oh, God, how my mother wished she hadn't inadvertently drugged and dragged me into this, before I was born.

Oh, God, how I wish my multigenerational maternal legacy didn't have such painful symmetries.

Oh, God, how I wish Eliana didn't have such painful asymmetry.

FIVE

In the Ramble this morning, I saw a red-tailed hawk capture and eat a squirrel. He sat in a tree, pinning the live squirrel to the branch with his talon, using his sharp beak to rip morsels of flesh from the dying animal, without apology or self-consciousness. Forever wild. This is the real thing, not an imitation of nature.

But the wild turkey is confused. He doesn't know his place in the natural world. He thinks he's a dog. He follows people in the Ramble, as if he were a pet. He prefers to follow men who are walking dogs. He stops when they stop, and sits tall, neck extended, facing straight ahead, imitating the dog. When dog and master start walking again, the turkey walks alongside them.

"When is Julia coming home?" Eliana asks at breakfast.

"Tuesday—"

"Yay!"

"For two days."

"Aw, that's such a short time."

"I know."

I wonder what it will be like having Julia back home. We've acclimated to being a family of three. She's just across the river, but it seems like she's so far away. I wonder if she's been in touch with her birth mother. And if so, what's that like? Is their relationship like a mother and daughter? Does it change how Julia sees me? I'd like to talk to Zoe, too, but I'm not sure Julia would want me to. What's the etiquette here? I've always wanted to see Zoe again. I was at the birth, I was with her during labor, I just about fell in love with her. But that's not the point. This is about Julia getting to know her birth mother. Another mother. A second mother, who was her original mother. Can we have too many mothers?

THE RADIATION ROOM is cool. The lights are dim. *Beep, beep, beep.*

"Please stay very still for ten minutes."

The labor room was cool. The lights were dim. Low, swooshing throb of Zoe's heartbeat, and quick liquid pulse of Baby's heart, whispered from the ultrasound heart monitor.

"Hey Alice, I'm really glad you're here," said Zoe. She was propped up in bed, the blue hospital gown over her round belly not quite covering her hips.

"Me, too." I was the only one in the room with her. Brad was in the waiting room. She had asked me to be her birth coach. I knew very little about childbirth, and I felt unprepared. An hour ago, we got the call from our social worker at the adoption agency, telling us that Zoe was in labor, and we cabbed down. The social worker bent the rules of the confidentiality agreement by telling us Zoe's last name, so that we could get into the hospital.

At the foot of Zoe's bed, a digital monitor displayed three wavy green lines.

"The top line is my contractions. It goes crazy when I'm in the middle of one. The second line is my heartbeat. The bottom line is the baby's heartbeat. Oh! Feel this."

Zoe grabbed my hand and put it on her round belly. I felt the baby kick. Then she groaned, gripped my hand, and described her sensations. She had opted not to have an epidural. Each contraction was more intense than the one before.

"I'm gonna be sick."

There was no nurse in sight. I grabbed a bucket. I was channeling my mother. I remembered Mom taking care of me when I was nauseous, feeding me crushed ice and ginger ale, propping me up, holding a bag for me to puke in, cleaning me up. I fed Zoe crushed ice from a paper cup. I held the plastic bucket for her. One time, Zoe missed the bucket and threw up on me. I cleaned up both of us. As the night wore on, as her contractions became more intense, I felt more and more like Zoe's mother, less and less like the baby's mother. Zoe was twenty, and she looked so young, it was confusing.

"Ready, Zoe?" asked the tall Jamaican midwife.

"I didn't know it would hurt this much. Can I have pain meds?"

"Too late for drugs. You can do it, girl. It's almost over," said the midwife, as we wheeled Zoe into the delivery room, where Brad, in green scrubs, awaited us.

Zoe pushed and pushed, until baby Julia dove magnificently into the world.

"Look at Alice and Brad," said Zoe, drenched in sweat but smiling. "They're crying because they're so happy."

Zoe chose me to be Julia's mother. I hope I've lived up to her expectations.

"Of course you have. You're a fine mother," says my mom.

"*Fine?* Fine isn't good enough."

"What's good enough?" She sits on the stool by the radiation bed, running her fingers through her salt-and-pepper hair. I have a sideways view of her, with my left cheek pressed to the mattress.

"Oh, God, that's what I'm trying to figure out, Mom. I think about Zoe. I love that girl—I mean, she's not a girl anymore, she's thirty-eight. She gave birth to Julia and then, miracle of miracles, she *gave* her baby to me and Brad. Literally placed newborn Julia in our arms. The greatest gift imaginable. I've been thankful—*indebted*—to Zoe every day of Julia's life. But now I'm worried that Julia will choose her over me. And Zoe might welcome that. Why wouldn't she? So I wonder, is Zoe a good mother to Julia? Has she been a good mother all along? When she was twenty and single, she knew she wasn't prepared to raise a child, so she made a carefully considered plan for her newborn. She chose loving parents for Julia, and disappeared from her life forever—anyway, that was her intent at the time. Until now, when she says,

"Wow, Julia, you found me! Cool—I'm here for you." So all this time, while she was waiting in the wings, was Zoe an ideal mother, in her own way? I think maybe yes. But mixed with my gratitude, I also feel a tinge of resentment. I can't help thinking about *The Little Red Hen.*

On cue, Mom, now much younger—black hair, red lips, slim waist—sits beside my bed and reads from my dog-eared storybook like she used to. The hen on the cardboard cover wears a yellow sweater and straw hat and plunges a spade into the ground with her strong chicken toes.

"'"Who will help me plant the wheat?" asks the Little Red Hen,'" Mom recites, in her mellifluous bedtime-story voice. "'"Not I," say all the animals in the farmyard." "Who will help me grind the wheat?" "Not I!"'" And so forth, and so on, blah, blah, blah . . ." Mom says, flipping pages to the end. "'"Who will help me bake the bread?" "Not I!" "And who will help me eat the bread?" "I will!" say all the animals.'"

"Exactly. And I confess to feeling, ungraciously, like the Little Red Hen. I raised Julia for eighteen years, and now that the hard work of parenting is done, Zoe gets to—you know—eat the bread."

My young mother laughs, her smile so pretty. "Or you

could say that Zoe planted the seed and baked the bread, and you're the one enjoying the fruits of *her* labor—pun intended. Pregnancy and childbirth are hard work."

"Well, yeah, point taken."

"You don't know what Zoe's expectations are. Or Julia's. She's not dumping you, she just wants to meet her birth mother."

"I know, I know. I'm ashamed of being so ungenerous."

"Guess you're not perfect, huh?"

MICHAEL, ELIANA, AND I went to Florida for the weekend, a quick visit with my dad and Jean, his wife of twenty-three years. Dad is ninety-three. (I have longevity and shortevity in my family.) He's slowing down. He has trouble walking, but he still plays piano every day, as well as he ever did, and he still has that charming, self-deprecating sense of humor. He even gets on a standing bike for ten minutes each morning, though he sometimes falls asleep in the middle of his workout. At ninety-three, he's more content than he has ever been. I'm happy that he's happy.

Dad is gradually letting go of things—sailing, walking, salty food, macho detachment, hearing in the upper range, stubborn self-sufficiency, short-term memory. He's replacing these old skills and habits with new ones—he's newly able to talk about feelings; he's learning to gracefully accept help; his memory keeps getting worse but it doesn't bother him much; he talks less, but he's more emotionally connected, more demonstrative; he cries easily. For the first time I can remember, he says, "I love you."

Oh, and yesterday, Zoe friended me on Facebook!

JULIA IS HOME! She got back at one in the morning. Night-owl Michael was still up. I got out of bed and sleepily joined the conversation, in a bit of a blur. "New friends . . . messy dorm room . . . math-obsessed roommate . . . phenomenal freshman seminar with the renowned Cornel West . . . rowing . . . a role in *Richard III*." She's in her world. She's happy and wildly enthusiastic about Princeton. I'm in a different place than she is, fretting about radiation and about Eliana's surgery. Our worlds don't yet mesh.

I'm glad Julia's here, but I'm distracted. She'll sleep late today. This morning, Eliana woke up and climbed under the covers in Julia's bed, and they hugged for a while. She went back to sleep when Eliana and I left for school. I'll take her out to lunch when I get back home from radiation. I hope she and Eliana have some time to hang out together. This is such a short visit.

Right before my senior year in college, I was briefly back home from an idyllic summer job in Martha's Vineyard, where I was the director of art and theater programs at the Chilmark Community Center. I had spent the summer living with other college students in a rustic farmhouse at Bliss Pond, just as blissful as its name.

There was a palpable but mystifying tension in my parents' house. I didn't want to know why. Icy chill between Mom and Dad. I could guess, but I didn't want evidence—too much responsibility. I preferred to play dumb. I was selectively open to conversation with my parents. They were selectively revealing and withholding. We tacitly agreed to this balancing act.

Jennifer had transformed, post braces, from Ugly Duckling to Beautiful Swan. She was suddenly gorgeous! My parents' rules and curfews, which I had deviously circumvented when I was in high school, were apparently no longer in place. Or my parents had given up trying to enforce them. Madeline had followed the rules.

I expended great effort surreptitiously breaking them. Jennifer made up her own.

On the desk of Mom's study, next to her old typewriter, was an imposing stack of feminist books. *Our Bodies, Our Selves* was on the bottom, the foundational tome. *Open Marriage* was conspicuously displayed on top of the pile.

I picked up the book and said, in the most raised-eyebrow, jokey tone I could muster, "So, are you and Dad into open marriage now?" which I immediately regretted, because she was going to respond as if it were a serious question.

She pushed her glasses up on her head, pursed her lips, tense and irritable, looked out the bay window at the great blue heron coming in for a landing on the salt marsh, and launched into a monologue.

"I wouldn't mind an open marriage," she said, "as long as it's equal, but there is no equity in marriage. There's a history in our culture—as there is in every culture—of wives getting the short end of the stick in every imaginable way. Income and property, for starters. Women's status in marriage hasn't really advanced since the Middle Ages."

"That's what my feminist theory professor says." I

offered, hoping to steer the conversation into more neutral territory, to no avail.

"Your professor is right. For example, your father owns this house, not me. I own nothing. Nothing. I've worked for thirty-five years, I've taught at universities and earned money for thirty-five years, and what do I have to show for it?"

Her voice got louder. She was no longer talking to me. I sat on the saggy daybed by the window and listened to a large moth flying into the screen, over and over, trying to get out. Mom paced the room, carrying *Open Marriage* and gesticulating with it.

"Even though I helped support our family, and even though I paid for your father to go to graduate school, and even though I did all the childcare and housework so that he could build his business, I'm not a stakeholder in this marriage. The whole institution of marriage is designed to keep women financially dependent and subservient. And when it comes to sexual politics? Please, don't get me started!"

"Okay, I won't."

But she'd already started, and there was no stopping her. I didn't know where she was going with this, but she was mad at men in general, and my parents weren't getting along. I was pretty sure Mom wanted to confide in me about something. I feared it was about my father having an affair. I hoped he wasn't, but if he was, I didn't want the burden of knowledge, even though I suspected it myself. Mom wanted my loyalty, but I wanted to be loyal to both Mom and Dad.

She plunked down next to me on the daybed, which bounced and sagged, knocking me off balance. I leaned on my right elbow.

"Suffice it to say—and you can draw your own conclusions—after I had cancer, after the double radical, my husband no longer saw me as a woman. Because, Alice, that's the way men are. And to tell you the truth, I no longer felt like a woman. We're trained to believe that our womanhood is defined by our external appearance. And when you lose your—Well. So. I've never talked about this with you before. It was excruciatingly difficult, still is. And your father . . ."

Her unfinished sentence was the open door for me to enter and invite her to tell me everything. I was torn. She'd never shared so much personal stuff with me. We hadn't been close for a very long time, and it was very tempting to step through that door and become her friend and confidant. She obviously wanted to tell me a secret, and that secret was undoubtedly about my father. But then I'd have to take sides, and I didn't want to side against Dad. The thought of it made my heart hurt.

She flipped through the pages of *Open Marriage*, without reading them. "Well. Hmm. You want my advice, Alice?"

"Okay."

"Don't get married."

"Do you really mean that?"

"Don't get married unless you want babies. And who wants babies?"

"That's weird advice, Mom."

"I'm kidding. I love my children."

"Glad to hear that."

"But if you *do* get married, *do not* put your husband through business school."

"O . . . kay . . . ?"

"It simply reinforces the status quo of financial inequality in this *lousy* institution. I was supporting our household, paying for my husband's tuition, taking care of babies, being a housewife, washing dishes. The dishes. The dishes! The goddamn dishes! No wonder women don't succeed."

"*Wonder Women* don't succeed?"

"What?"

"It's a joke, Mom. *Wonder Woman.* The comic super-hero? Never mind. You were saying?"

"Women don't succeed, because we're up to our el-bows in dishwater."

"I know what you mean, Mom." I felt a pang of guilt, suddenly remembering that time, years ago, when we gave her a broom and a dustpan for Mother's Day. How could we have been so stupid?

"By the time you three babies were out of diapers and I finally got back to writing, so much time had passed that what I had written was out of date. Every time I read over a new draft, I'd outgrown the damn thing. The goddamn dishes keep us from writing fast enough to make a mark in the world."

"Wow. That's a really interesting concept."

"We make a pittance while our husbands get rich. When the woman gets older and the sexual attraction is gone, what was all that sacrifice for?"

"I don't know."

"Exactly! So my advice, Alice, is don't get married unless you find someone who doesn't buy the old rules, because the old rules stink!"

"Got it. And that's good advice."

She got up and paced the room again, glancing at me to deliver her main points, as if this were a lecture hall and I was her only student. It was dusk, and the crickets were singing.

"I used to be called an eccentric. Now I'm called a feminist! It's a wonderful thing. For the first time, I'm professionally valued for my life experience as a wife-slash-mother-slash-housewife-slash-perpetual PhD candidate. This new role legitimizes that which previously was assigned zero value."

"That's cool."

"I gave a talk to a group of women at the library last week. I said, 'I had an *epiphany* on the tennis court! My husband and I have always played tennis together. Whenever a new racket came on the market, he bought the new racket and I got his old one. His game kept getting better. Mine stayed the same. This year, my husband got a *Prince* and his game improved dramatically. And I said, impulsively, "Ira, I want a Prince." After a moment's pause, he said, "Okay." And I bought a Prince. Voila! My tennis game improved.'"

"What was your epiphany?"

"That all these years, I could have been improving my tennis game, like my husband. And I began to think of all the areas of my life where I have settled for leftovers, hand-me-downs, second bests, and how much I could have improved—and still can improve—if I stop settling."

"That's great. Mom. You always taught us to challenge the status quo. I'm proud of you."

She sat on the creaky daybed again and looked at me. My heart hurt again.

"I thought I might talk to you about something . . ." she said, pausing long enough for me to consider saying, *What do you want to talk about, Mom? You can tell me anything.* But I didn't say a word, and the unspoken *something* remained suspended in the ellipsis, until the moment passed and the silence became awkward.

It was getting darker. She got up, turned on a lamp, and rummaged around the clutter on her desk. "Alice, did you see where I put my glasses?"

"They're on your head."

"Ah."

This was my chance to open up to her, invite her to talk to me. She initiated this, and now the ball was in my court. It could be a turning point for us, a new beginning. But then I might have been obligated to reject my Dad, and I didn't want to take that risk. Anyway, Mom had close friends her own age she could confide in.

The moth was still throwing himself into the screen, *ping, ping, ping . . .*

"I should start packing for school."

"Yes, of course."

At the end of the week in the new house—which would never feel like home, because I had hardly lived there, except for a couple of weeks each summer before college—I went back to school.

My sisters swing by after work to say hi to Julia before she heads back to school. Madeline, Jennifer, and I are best friends, even closer as adults than we were as children, and they're both stellar aunts to my girls. Madeline has been consulting with Eliana on her Halloween costume. She has a master's degree in costume design and I can barely thread a needle, so I leave the execution of this project to them. They disappear into Ellie's room to add the finishing touches, while Julia, Jennifer, and I make dinner and schmooze in the kitchen.

Eliana emerges to model the craziest costume I have ever seen—"I'm half Voldemort, half umbrella." Her long hair is tightly pulled back under a white bathing cap, and her face is painted white, with black slits for

Voldemort's serpentine, noseless nostrils. She wears an umbrella hat and a long black robe, with an aluminum-foil umbrella handle sewn on the front. Hilarious and creepy. She takes a bow. We applaud and laugh and agree that while there will be loads of Harry Potter characters trick-or-treating tomorrow, she'll be the only Voldebrella.

After dinner, Julia slings her Princeton Crew bag over her shoulder (now that she's an athlete, she's got tons of swag). Eliana reaches up and Julia reaches down, folding her long arms around her little sister. They hold each other for a long time. "I gotta go, Eliana," whispers Julia, gently.

I ASK MY sisters about our childhood.

"For the most part," says Madeline, "I remember growing up being a pretty happy-go-lucky time."

I laugh.

"Why are you laughing?"

"Did you really say 'happy-go-lucky'?"

"Yes, that's how I remember it."

"No way."

"*Yes* way!"

"I thought you were being ironic." I stifle my laughter. I'm amazed.

"But you know me—my credo is, avoid negative thoughts at all costs," she adds, with a touch of self-mocking humor that I find reassuring. "It wasn't *all* great. Dad and Mom argued a lot. And Mom had all those phobias. She was afraid of mountain roads and open windows and thunder and elevators and sharks and the ocean. There was a year when she was agoraphobic. And she was so indecisive and so overprotective that it drove me crazy. It was mortifying when she'd march into school in curlers and a raincoat over her nightgown, to give the principal a piece of her mind."

"Now *that* I remember exactly the same way."

"And there were all these race issues in our neighborhood. Starting in junior high, I was passionate about the civil rights movement. In eleventh grade I went to the prom with a black guy, and a few days later, I overheard a classmate saying, 'Madeline went to the prom with a nigger.' But I had already established myself as a marginal, lefty, high-achieving nerd, so I guess that insulated me. And I had my friends. So I stand by my statement. All in all, my childhood was happy-go-lucky."

(I guess I don't have the happy-go-lucky gene.)

"I wish I kept at least some of Mom's writing," I say. "Dad was in such a hurry to clear out the house after she died. I feel terrible that we dumped her papers. Boxes and boxes, thousands of pages. I can't believe it's all gone."

"I have her masters thesis from Columbia," says Madeline.

"Really?" I'm stunned.

"Yeah," she says, "You want it?"

"Yes! Definitely. Thank you."

"I remember having a very happy childhood, being loved and cared for in a fun and happy home," says Jennifer. "It's hard for me to believe that you have those negative memories and feelings about Mom. I put her on a pedestal. She loved and protected us so intensely—she was like a mother bird who would peck the eyes out of anyone who hurt her babies, she loved us that much. And I saw how different and awful it could be for the other kids in our neighborhood. Rosalia's father beat her and her siblings with a belt on a regular basis; in second grade I saw him throw his wife down the stairs. And it was just terrible the way my friend Emma's mother told her she couldn't play with me anymore, because all Jews had bedbugs. So, in contrast to my friends, whose parents were so cruel and violent, I felt safe and cared for. It was hard to compete with my big sisters for Mom and Dad's attention, but I knew we would always be protected and loved by our parents."

Wow, okay. I remember all these awful things Jennifer described. And I, too, remember feeling loved and cared for in a fun, happy home—that is, when I was a little girl. In adolescence? Not so much. I'm perversely envious that the cruelty Jennifer observed in the neighborhood underscored for her how wonderful our family life was in contrast; whereas, from my camera angle, they reinforce my memory of our neighborhood as a hostile place.

My sisters and I are best friends. We grew up in the same house, in the same neighborhood, with the same parents. But we perceived it all so differently while growing up, and we remember it so differently as adults. Why? Genetic predisposition? Birth order? Circumstance? Chance? How significant was it that Mom's losing her breasts coincided with my breasts developing? Madeline was at college at that time, and Jennifer was still a little girl, so Mom's illness didn't affect them as dramatically. For me, it was a tectonic shift, which caused a tsunami of tension between me and Mom.

SIX

Dr. Giordano warned me that the last week of radiation was the worst, and that the symptoms would get progressively worse for a couple of weeks following treatment. I apologize to Eliana for not hugging her (because it hurts), and then regret mentioning it when she says, "That's okay, Mom. It's embarrassing when you hug me in front of my friends. I only do it because I know you like it." Ouch and ouch.

It takes them forever to position me. Reggie and Jamal push and prod my back and ribs, which hurts. I try to lie passively. I'm dead weight. They seem unable to move me. And the skin on my left breast is burning, burning.

I can't think about anything but breasts.

When I was twelve and my breasts first started developing, they felt like apricots, and I loved touching them at night under the sheets.

La la la la la la la la la la la la la la la la la la la la la la
la la la la la la la la la la la la la la la la la la la la la la la
la la la la la la la la la la la la la la la la la la la la la la

Still not over.

A Short History of Breasts (my mother's and mine): My mother didn't breastfeed; it was out of fashion. When I gave birth, breastfeeding was back in fashion, but I was a flop. The whole freaking La Leche League couldn't figure out how to get my *leche* to flow. The sublime utility of breasts, ever since the first mammal secreted milk, two hundred million years ago. The futility of mine—and of my mother's. Our utter udder failure. Except as an erogenous zone. In that context, I have enjoyed outstanding form and function, for four decades and counting. Oh, yes. Yes. YES, GOD, YES!

Ouch, ouch, ouch, poor left breast.

I think about other women's breasts. In the movies, in the locker room, roommates, friends, that nude beach. All varieties of beautiful. I picture women and their bare breasts in myriad shapes and sizes.

Damn. I want to get this over with.

How 'bout that time when my friend Hinda, the co-founder and president of JogBra, enlisted me as her model for "BigBra," a new product for big-breasted joggers. I met her on the Lower East Side, where her tailor, Shlomo, fitted me, and together we designed a Nobel Prize–worthy bra that would enable buxom women the world over to jog in comfort.

Longest ten minutes ever. Aarrgh!

As my treatments are nearing the end, I meet with Eliana's teacher, Cindy Swan, to line up our ducks.

"How long will Eliana be out of school?"

"It's hard to predict. Depends how she deals with the pain. We think she'll be home for about six weeks, till right after the New Year. When she goes back, will she have a paraprofessional to help her get around the school safely?"

"It's already in our system."

"She's worried about returning to school using a walker. She'll be self-conscious if other kids stare at her."

"She can always talk to me about it."

"This will be really hard for Eliana." I fight back tears. She pushes the box of tissues toward me. "It'll work out."

"Eliana," Dr. Campbell said cheerfully, when we met him almost a year ago, "you're lucky that leg-lengthening is an option." He grabbed a fake fractured femur from his windowsill display of artificial bones encased in metal scaffolding, and brandished it with manly brio, looking like a high-tech caveman. "Until recently, limb-lengthening was considered a medical impossibility, except in Siberia. After World War II, hidden behind the wall of the Cold War, Dr. Ilizarov discovered bone-lengthening, by accident.

"Dr. Ilizarov instructed one of his patients to tighten a screw every day for two weeks, on a device meant to straighten his fractured knee. But the guy accidentally turned the screw the wrong way. Two weeks later, he was surprised to find that the patient had lengthened his own leg.

"From this lucky accident—not so lucky for that fellow, but lucky for you, Eliana—Ilizarov discovered bone's capacity to create new bone.

"This is what *your* fixator will look like," he said, handing Eliana another fractured femur—this one with a long metal rod screwed into it with six large bolts. "Do you have any questions?"

Eliana stared at the impaled bone in her hands. "Um . . . Will my life be different, I mean, like on an everyday basis?"

"Yes. You won't be running around, jumping, skipping, or climbing for a few months."

"Can I go to gym class?"

"No."

"Will I miss any school?"

"Yes. Some kids go back to school a week after surgery. Other kids need a few weeks or a few months. Every child is different."

"Cool! I get to miss school! When will I be a hundred percent better?"

"It takes eight months."

"Let's just get it over with," she said.

Dr. Campbell was pleased that she was so agreeable. But the casual bravura of her "Let's get it over with" told me that she envisioned this as a mere inconvenience. I'd heard from other parents about the months of pain and incapacitation. I didn't want to rush into an irrevocable decision.

Dr. Campbell countered my furrowed brow with a raised eyebrow, which I translated to mean, *Unfurrow your brow, Mom! This is as much as we can tell an eight-year-old. We don't want to scare her out of having surgery. She's too young to imagine how painful this procedure really is. She said, 'Let's get it over with,' and*

that's as much as we can ask of her right now. Children
are resilient. She'll get through this. Trust me.

Our eyebrow dialogue persuaded me to trust him. Until he added:

"In my opinion, any parent who doesn't have their
child's leg lengthened—when they have the option—is
guilty of child abuse."

His statement had the opposite of its intended effect.
It made me wonder if subjecting my child to this tor-
turous procedure was a form of child abuse. I resented
his damning insinuation about any parent who hesitates,
who questions, who has the audacity to consider that surgery for a non-life-threatening condition may not be right
for their child.

The absolute certainty of his statement about parental
guilt was even more infuriating, in light of the several
times in my life when doctors have made declarations
of absolute and unassailable truth—which have sub-
sequently turned out to be absolutely and unassailably
false. (Case in point: my pregnancy with Eliana, which
three doctors and four radiologists misdiagnosed for six
months as everything *but* a pregnancy.)

"When modern medicine affords children this opportunity to improve the quality of their lives, parents who
stand in the way . . ."

The more he talked, the angrier I got. I began to feel like my mother, enraged on her daughter's behalf at some real or imagined injustice. I pictured Mom storming into my high school in a raincoat over a nightgown, demanding "a word with the principal," earning a reputation as "an irate parent" and "Alice's crazy mother," humiliating me in the process. I didn't want to do that to Eliana. Maybe I was getting a little carried away. I had to believe that Dr. Campbell had Eliana's best interests at heart.

"I just want to get it over with," Eliana repeated, handing the fake bone back to the surgeon and defusing our eyebrow standoff.

SEVEN

I finish reading Mom's master's thesis, written for her degree in Public Law and Government from Columbia University. Her study, *The Politics of Housing in a Suburban Community*, analyzes how the many factions within our town of Mamaroneck perceived a politically charged issue in entirely different ways: an urban renewal project, fought over for years, and ultimately rejected. After a fire ripped through a tenement building that was home to low-income immigrant and minority families, a housing project was proposed as a remedy for substandard housing in the town. The proposal inflamed tensions across the ideological spectrum.

THE FLICKERING CANDLELIGHT bounces off the red and gold walls, casting a warm glow in the restaurant. The turbaned sitar player closes his eyes, while the tabla player takes a solo, synchronizing his drumming to intricate vocals, alternating seven-beat and eight-beat patterns, articulated at lightning speed—*TakKiTa/TaKiTa/TaKa, TakKiTa/TaKiTa/TaKa, TaKiTa/TaKa/DiMi, TaKiTa/TaKa/DiMi, TaKa/TaKiTa/TaKa/TaKiTa/TaKa/DiMi, TaKa/TaKiTa/TaKa/TaKiTa/TaKa/DiMi.* His staccato syllables command attention. There's a hush in the restaurant, until the sitar player starts up again, then the festive din of conversation resumes.

Mom sits across the table from me, in one of her *ethnic shmatas*—that's what she calls her loose-fitting Indian print dresses she's taken to wearing—and a long, beaded necklace. "I'm in a good mood, and I'd like a beer," she muses. The waiter instantly appears with two Kingfisher beers.

"Cheers!" We clink bottles and drink.

"Belated congratulations. I just read your master's thesis, and it's, well, kind of amazing."

"Goodness gracious, you read that? The whole kit and caboodle?"

"Yup."

She blushes, puts her hands on her flushed cheeks. "I'm honored. It's not exactly easy reading."

"No, but it's fascinating." I pull the hundred-page

manuscript from my purse and lay it on the table in front of her.

She puts on her bifocals and picks it up. "I haven't seen this since—well, it's dated 1965. I conducted the research from 1961 to 1965, from the time you were—seven to eleven years old."

"I heard your voice when I read it, and I want to talk to you about it tonight. I don't know if we'll see each other again."

"Of course we will," Mom says, flipping through the pages. "Are these your pencil marks or mine?"

"Mine. This is a photocopy. I wouldn't write on the original."

"*Pff,* why not? It's been gathering dust for half a century. How gratifying that someone has actually read it—that *you've* read it. I'm terribly flattered. Thank you, Sweetheart, this is a lot of fun for me. Let's see what I wrote. I hope it's not all drivel and nonsense." She reads aloud. "'*It was a conflict on a small scale. But the particular issue of public housing acted with centrifugal force—whirling outward from the central question was a vast field of conflicting values, rights, and interests.*' That is precisely what it was like, Alice. Centrifugal force— a cyclone. '*There is no precise beginning or end to the story*'—Is there ever?" (She flips pages to the next highlighted passage, nodding in agreement with her own words.) "'. . . *It is difficult to precisely define social groups or classes. As a family's income increases, as it moves upward and outward away from its former home, the life style changes. Class seems not so much a collective unity, but a suspension of attitudes, values, aspiration— linked to the past, listing to the future—where each family is perched in the community web, at a given point in time.*'"

I laugh. "Those are the same big words that went over my head when I was a kid. I underlined that section because it resonated with my confusion about our family's social class while I was growing up."

"Well, of course it would. Our family existed in a volatile place in that community web, eluding easy class definition. What's next? Ah. *'The insulation of life in suburbia, in separate neighborhoods, would seem to be of a higher order than that in central city areas'*—I'll say it was insulated! Blah blah blah, skip that, skip that—*'In suburbia, one can function to a large extent within an orbit of one's school, church, shopping area, social club, and train, without too often crossing another neighborhood or other ways of life.'*"

"Were you writing about your own frustration with suburban life?"

"I wasn't writing about myself. I'm a social scientist."

"I know that. Sorry if it seems—"

"But God, yes, there were times when I thought I'd suffocate in our town. You're wise to raise your family in the city—it's good for you and it's good for your kids, and for your husband."

"Thank you."

"What did I write next? Blah blah blah . . . *'The athletic and social societies of the well-to-do, the golf, beach, and yacht clubs, are separated quite precisely according to religion: Catholic, Protestant, and Jewish'*—Did you know that your father was not allowed to join the yacht club? —*'The Negroes are conspicuously absent from these sports activities. . . . The number of associations is astounding. They whirl within the community like so many self-propelled satellites.'* My guess is that it still pertains today. Who knew my paper would hold up nearly fifty years later?"

The waiter brings two more Kingfishers. We clink and drink.

"I really like what you said about the *theys* in this next section. It's completely relevant today. And it resonates with my childhood perception of racism and anti-Semitism in our neighborhood."

She nods to herself, while she reads aloud, and the tabla player matches her syllables and her nodding with his drumming. "'. . . *The community is fragmented into many small sub-groups whose views of each other are seen as if through a prism: a set of distortions, a mosaic of images of "they," as perceived by those in the varying strata of the community. As you speak with individuals, there is a constant use of the personal referent 'they.' The 'theys' in the community are ranked in an intricate and precise patterning. And depending upon the position of the individual, the "they" may be ranked either above or below one. . . ."They" has an important function in camouflaging remarks that might otherwise be considered inflammatory and discriminatory. It also involves the listener in a conspiracy of silent acceptance of the "right" way of doing things. For example, no one in public speaks of the Negroes or Jews. What one can say is 'they' don't live the same way you or I do.'"*

"In our neighborhood, our family was the *they*."

"Yes, Alice, that's right. . . . I was a complete outsider, because I didn't conform to the narrowly defined codes of behavior. Did you as a child ever feel like a *they* in our neighborhood?"

"Most of the time."

"Oh dear, I'm sorry. That must have been very lonely for you." She flips more pages. *"In effect, the myriad municipalities in the metropolitan area act like tiny city-states—carefully drawing economic and color barricades around their boundaries; exercising their sovereignty, protecting their limited resources via zoning and building codes and the unwritten covenants of discrimination.'"*

"Reading your thesis last night, Mom, it all made sense to me, looking back."

"The five of us lived in the same little house for the four years that I was analyzing the politics of our town, all of us experiencing it differently. What were we each doing during that time?

"You were typing."

"Ira was sailing."

"Madeline was having fun with her friends."

"Jennifer was my happy little girl—at least I think she was."

"And I felt like was standing in the crossfire of a dangerous battlefront."

"Always?"

"No, but it often seemed like I lived in that tiny city-state you described."

"You modeled yourself after me, Alice. Walked in my

footsteps, for better or worse, by choosing the vantage point of a pint-sized social scientist. You observed our striated, factionalized neighborhood, with its ethnic, religious, racial, socioeconomic boundaries, just like I did."

"Not *just* like you. My technique was different. I climbed the tree and spied on you guys—"

"You spied on us?"

"Yup."

She laughs. "Good for you, for discovering an original method for conducting fieldwork. I'm starving. Let's order dinner." She finishes the second bottle of beer and waves to the waiter.

THAT NIGHT, MICHAEL, Eliana, and I stay up late and watch the election coverage. I feel bad sending Eliana to bed at midnight, before the results are in. She cries and storms, but it's a school night and it's already way past her bedtime. Michael and I stay up. It's a thrilling night. When I finally go to sleep, I feel more patriotic than I have ever felt before. Obama's election would have made my mother so happy.

EIGHT

....

"Is your cancer cured now, Mom?"

"I think so, yes."

"That's great!" Eliana throws her arms around me. I wince, but don't tell her how much it hurts.

"Mom, when is my surgery?"

"In thirteen days."

"That's soon."

"Yeah."

The school bell rings, and she sprints into the building.

IT'S MY LAST treatment.

I'm going to miss Jamal and Reggie.

I am going to miss the women in the waiting room. We sit around in our gowns reading women's magazines. We wish each other luck. Patients come and go—younger and older than me. Some have both radiation and chemo, some just radiation. Some of us will survive. You get to know someone on your first day here, and she finishes treatment when you're in the middle of yours, and someone new shows up. The magazines don't change, so we tell each other which articles are our favorites. Six weeks ago, I was the new one in the room. The more seasoned radiation patients gave me tips.

"Take naps every day."

"Take warm baths with scented candles."

"Read this inspiring article in *Oprah* magazine by a breast cancer survivor."

Now, I'm one of the experienced patients, giving tips to the newbies.

"Try walking through the Ramble in Central Park. And read this inspiring article in *Oprah* magazine."

THERE IS THE customary sound of the low drone and rhythmic beeps, the hum of the fan and the muffled chords of classical music. The robotic arm of the radiation machine makes her slow circle one last time, hovering above me, smoothly arcing to the right, hovering at my side.

And now my mother's arm encircles me. I don't see her, but I feel the warmth of her arm reaching around me.

"I'm going to miss you, Mom. I mean, I'll miss having you in the room with me. I'm grateful for these ten-minute interludes that have conjured our reunion, and for the flood of memories I'd blocked out for so long and that came back with such force. But Mom, when this last session is over, I won't want you with me anymore. It's time for me to concentrate on very real maternal responsibilities. I'll need to focus on Eliana and getting her through this difficult procedure."

"I could help you with that."

"What makes you think I need your help?"

"You invited me."

"Why did I do that?"

"You want my advice."

"Okay, give me a quick synopsis, before the ten minutes are up."

"Don't try to be a perfect mother."

"I reject that advice. Because—sorry if this offends you—I want to be a better mother than you were."

"Maybe you will be, but there's no such thing as a perfect mother."

"Okay, not perfect. Unambivalent."

"Good luck with that!" she laughs. "You are your mother's daughter."

"Okay, okay. Unwavering, then."

"We all waver. Every mother fails her child at some point. I did. You did. Zoe did. The kids turn out okay."

"I guess so."

"If you try to be perfect—"

"Please, Mom, I want you to leave before Eliana has surgery."

"—you'll end up letting everybody down—"

"Or I'll get really confused."

"—including yourself."

"Are you sure I invited you? I don't remember inviting you."

"This will help you to remember."

I feel my mother's hands on my back, X marks the spot, with a dot, dot, dot, and I do remember. Her hands are so warm. She's teaching me to knead dough, she combs my hair, she sings a lullaby, she's laughing, she's admiring my drawings and paintings, she makes chicken soup, she brings a gray kitten home for me after I have chicken pox, she makes oatmeal cookies, she leads my Camp Fire Girl group on a hiking trip, she watches Julia Child on television and makes us boeuf bourguignon, she strokes my back, with a dash and a line and a big question mark, she throws salt over her shoulder for good luck, the air tastes like salt, everything is salty, like tears, like the ocean, like wind over waves at the beach, trickle up, trickle down, trickle all around, and I want the trickle up trickle down part to last forever.

"*We are finished, Ms. Cohen. You may move about.*"

"Are you alright?" Reggie asks, after I pull my robe on.

"I'm fine," I say, wiping my tear-streaked cheeks.

"Don't take this the wrong way, Ms. Cohen," says Jamal, "but we hope we never have to see you again."

FOR TWO WEEKS after radiation ends, I'm wiped out, as predicted. My radiated skin looks and feels like it's sunburned. It peels off in small strips. Underneath the peeling skin are patches of brand-new pale pink, damp skin. Itching and stinging. Cool baths help, for the duration of the bath. When I finish molting, the new skin on my left breast is pink and tender, like a newborn's. My treatment is finished, except for tamoxifen, the estrogen blocker I'll start next month and continue for five years.

"Mommy, when is my surgery?"

"The day after tomorrow."

"I'm scared."

"I know."

My heart sinks lower and lower in my chest, as if weighted down with lead weights, like the ones Daddy and I tied onto string to fish for bottom-feeding flounders.

My weighted heart sinks all the way down and lies in the sand under the sea.

I reach for Michael's hand, in bed, late at night.

"Michael, I'm scared of Eliana's surgery. Are we doing the right thing?"

"Yes."

"What if something goes wrong?"

"We'll deal with it."

"What if it's too much for her to bear?"

"It won't be."

"I'm having second thoughts."

"You always have second thoughts."

"How do we know it's the right thing to do?"

"Because three doctors said she needs this surgery."

"How do we know those three doctors are right?"

"How do we know anything?"

"I don't want to do it."

"I can't take your waffling, Alice."

"I'm having really strong second thoughts."

"Don't let Eliana know that."

"Okay. But I can't stop feeling that it's a mistake."

"Get over it. Eliana's having surgery the day after tomorrow."

PART 3

....

"Never say good-bye because good-bye means
going away and going away means forgetting."

—J. M. BARRIE, *Peter Pan*

ONE

. . . .

"You look like a snowman," Eliana said groggily, while she was still conscious. I was wearing a billowy white coverall, surgical mask, slippers, and hairnet. "You should wear that for Halloween."

"I will," I promised.

I held her hand as she was rolled into the presurgery room. She was hooked up to an IV and quickly going under, her eyelids fluttering. "I love you," I whispered, kissing her forehead.

There was no turning back.

I joined Michael in the waiting room, and we stared out the picture window at the red sunrise over the ice-capped East River.

"I wish we'd braided her hair," I said hoarsely, after a few silent minutes.

"I was just thinking that," said Michael.

"No clips or rubber bands allowed," the nurse told us. "Just pile her hair up in the net." But I knew how tangled Eliana's long, thick hair could get, and I regretted not braiding it. I also regretted . . . I suppressed the thought. There were steps I could take to repair tangled hair. My other misgivings were without remedy and therefore pointless to dwell on. So I obsessed about her unbraided hair and drank bitter waiting-room coffee.

An hour passed, and Dr. Campbell appeared.

"The surgery went like clockwork!" he proudly announced.

Michael and I held hands as we walked into the recovery room, cheerful as a morgue. Unconscious men and women lay in two rows of beds, tethered to breathing tubes and IVs.

Eliana was the only child. She looked like a beautiful fairytale princess who wound up in the wrong story. Her face was pale and still. We sat and waited and watched. Finally, her eyelids flickered and her fingers twitched. As she awakened, she was animated, surprisingly cheerful, kind of loopy. I was glad we'd prepared her for the discombobulating experience of waking with no sensation in her legs. She delivered a slightly demented and very funny running commentary on her sensations and lack thereof. She made us laugh.

But when the anesthesia wore off, she felt the bulky metal rod on her right leg. She realized that her thigh was impaled, through flesh and into bone, with six long bolts, which fastened the heavy fixator to her. She realized that this contraption would be attached to her leg for six months, and that she couldn't move her leg without intense pain.

"I wouldn't have done it, if I knew it would hurt this much," she sobbed.

Eliana wanted to forget the four terrible days and nights she spent in the hospital: the pain and dislocation, the excruciating hours of physical therapy. I felt responsible for her agony, and regretted everything. Michael wanted me to stop my self-reproach, for God's sake, and move on.

Eliana's hair was so tangled by the first night that it was impossible to comb without causing more pain, so we postponed the inevitable task. The second day, her hair was a single dreadlock. The third day, her locks were more tightly locked, her dread more dreadful. On the fifth day, the physical therapist on staff said Eliana had made sufficient progress to be released from the hospital.

THE ORDERLY HELPS us get into a cab. The three of us squeeze into the back seat and hold hands. Eliana's pediatric-sized walker—with which she is able to take a few painful, hesitant steps—lies folded on the floor in front of her. The taxi careens through Central Park and takes us home.

TWO

Eight months, for an eight-year-old girl, might as well be forever. The doctor said she had to begin weight-bearing immediately, even though each step is painful. This is more terrible than Eliana could have imagined. This is exactly as terrible as I had imagined. This is precisely the manageable challenge Michael had imagined.

Unlike me, Michael is not collapsing into a puddle of emotional ineptitude. He's on top of it. He remains even-keeled, matter-of-fact. He deals with everything. He's a rock. He's the man. He's the father. He sometimes has to be the mother, since I'm too incapacitated by sadness and fear and regret to be of much use. So much for my goal of maternal perfection.

Before the operation, Eliana was private and modest. She would get upset if I inadvertently opened the door while she was getting dressed. Now, she has to compartmentalize her modesty. She closes the door when she dresses herself in the morning, but accepts, resignedly, that Michael has to bathe her every night. I'm not strong enough to pick her up. Michael lifts her into the tub, carefully seats her on the plastic stool, and bathes her with the hand-held showerhead we installed before the operation. She wraps herself in a towel while he cleans the six pin-sites on her thigh, where the fixator is attached, with a mixture of hydrogen peroxide and saline solution—literally pouring salt into her wounds. With six holes in her leg, infection is a constant danger, and Michael is vigilant.

If only I could kiss her boo-boo and make it better. I try to do the pin care, but when she cries, "It hurts so much, please stop, please stop!" I stop. It's a reflex. I can't continue when my child cries.

Eliana is able to temporarily lose herself in movies and television. She watches every episode of *The Brady Bunch* and *Little House on the Prairie,* and countless hours of *SpongeBob SquarePants.* On the third day home, I ask her to choose a movie so I can attend to the one problem I know I can fix. While she's reviewing her options, I run across the street to the small salon where Ahmed cuts my hair.

"Try this," says Ahmed, handing me a large bottle of extra-strength detangler, "And this." He grabs a jar of hair goo from a high shelf. "Comb one small strand at a time, starting at the ends and slowly moving up to the scalp."

"Thanks, Ahmed. How much do I owe you?"

"Nothing. Just tell your daughter to get better, and bring her in if you need my help."

Grateful for his kindness, I race back with the loot.

"I chose *The Wizard of Oz*."

"Focus on the movie and pay no attention to me." I liberate one strand at a time, while Dorothy survives a tornado, vanquishes the Witch, and outs the Wizard. By the third click of her ruby slippers, the tangles are out.

Eliana refuses to take pain medication. I stroke her back to help her fall asleep, trying to channel my mother's expert touch. "X marks the spot, with a dot, dot, dot, and a dash and a line, and a big question mark. Trickle up, trickle down, trickle all around, with a pinch and a squeeze, and a cool ocean breeze."

"Again, Mommy," she murmurs half-asleep, reminding me of myself as a child.

"X marks the spot with a dot, dot, dot . . ." I can comb her tangles and give her back rubs, but I can't make her better. I'm too weak and too squeamish to give her the medical care she needs. Michael is in charge of that. I'm merely his assistant, his sous-chef. It isn't enough.

When she's asleep, I swallow my first dose of tamoxifen. I put the pill bottle back, close the medicine cabinet, glance at the mirror, and see my mother's face.

In a panic, I swing open the door of the medicine cabinet, so I can't see the mirror. I distractedly rearrange the clutter of antacids, tamoxifen, Band-Aids, and pain meds, and sit down on the edge of the tub, my heart pounding.

Why is she here? I told her to stay away, that I didn't want her around right now.

Yes, I want to remember my mother. I miss our talks and those radiation sessions, when we were transported back in time. But I refuse to be literally haunted by her. Mom wouldn't have believed in this version of herself— showing up as a ghost in my bathroom mirror. She adamantly did not believe in an afterlife. No heaven, no eternal spirit, no ghosts, no angels, no visitations. "I want to be cremated," she said, though her wish was trumped by her father's wish for her to have a Jewish burial. "When you die, the body is meaningless, except that it makes excellent fertilizer. New flowers will grow where old ashes are buried," she told me. She subscribed to no concept of a hereafter, except for her pantheistic belief that everything and everyone is part of one infinitely connected Cosmos, guided by Mother Nature. She herself wouldn't endorse this vision of her ghostly face in the mirror being anything but a product of my imagination. She can't be here. She has to leave.

I slowly close the medicine cabinet—and see only my own face.

I look older. I'm beginning to look like my mother. I stare at my silvering hair, the circles under my eyes. When did I get this old?

I turn from the mirror. This is not the time to dwell on mortality.

THREE

Eliana's classmates send her an enormous get-well card. Her teachers send her a cookie telegram. Madeline sends books. Jennifer sends her a sock-puppet-making kit.

She gets a stomach flu. She grips her walker and slowly shuffles back and forth between living room and bathroom many times a day. No one can visit. She's lonely and sad.

A week after her surgery, we begin to lengthen her leg, one millimeter a day. We do this by fitting an L-shaped Allen wrench onto the bottom bolt of her metal fixator, and turning it ninety degrees, four times a day. It is astoundingly low-tech. Eliana often lengthens her own leg. It takes only a few seconds to turn the wrench 90 degrees, and—*Voila!*—the leg is a quarter of a millimeter longer. After the fourth turn of each day, her leg is one millimeter longer; in ten days, a centimeter. After seven weeks, her right leg will be five centimeters longer, about two inchs. At the end of the whole procedure, she'll still need a one-inch shoe lift, down from her current three-inch lift.

The quarter-turns don't hurt. But the cumulative impact of this rapid elongation of her leg, soft tissue and bone, does hurt. Bending her leg at the knee—supervised by me, Michael, and the physical therapist who comes to our apartment daily—is terribly painful.

Eliana is missing all the classroom prep for the fourth-grade test. We hire a tutor to prepare Eliana for the high-stakes citywide exam in January, which determines where kids will be admitted to middle school.

Katherine is smart in a bookish way and attractive in a goth way. But she has, among other problems, a deeply embedded *I don't really like children, and I dislike their parents even more* problem.

"We need to be alone!" she snarls, shutting the door and forbidding us to enter the living room. We mistake this for intellectual rigor.

At Katherine's second visit, she hands Eliana four stapled pages just before she leaves. "Make sure Eliana completes these sample test questions before my next visit," she says sternly, buckling her black leather coat before vanishing into the overcast, wintry afternoon.

"Mom, what does this mean?" asks Eliana, poring over Katherine's printout.

"They're sample test questions."

"No, I mean the stuff on the back of the pages."

I take the stapled packet from her. Good grief! Printed on the back is a pornographic story, graphically describing Katherine's experiences as a dominatrix.

"Oh, my God! I can't believe she gave this to you."

"What does it say?"

"I can't tell you what it says, it's so inappropriate."

"But it's mine!" She grabs for the stapled pages, which I hold out of reach. "It's mine! She gave it to me, Mom."

Julia, home from Princeton for winter break, takes the pages from my hand and holds them even higher above Eliana's reach.

"Oh! My! God!" says Julia, giggling as she reads. "This is unbelievable!"

"I want to read it!" says Eliana.

"No way!" says Julia.

No more tutoring.

WHY DID WE fix what ain't broke? It's certainly broke now.

"Nobody prepared me for this," Eliana says, and I can only nod in agreement.

Her ambulatory skill improves, but she says the walker makes her feel like an old person. I understand. The sound of her tentative footstep alternates with the dull thud of the walker.

"I'm not myself anymore. I feel like I've lost myself and will never be myself again." She wishes she could tear out the fixator. "I can't be my real self with this thing in my leg." She can't roll over in bed. She can't wear pants. Even the oversized, snap-up sports pants don't cover the heavy strip of metal that extends several inches past her knee when she sits down.

There's no turning back.

Eliana is depressed.

It seems terribly wrong for my eight-year-old to be depressed. Since I can't do the pin care, I should be able to help her with her depression—I've been there, I'm the resident expert. But I don't know what to do, other than listen when she talks, worry about her without telling her I'm worried, empathize with her, schedule physical therapy and doctor visits, dispense hugs and back rubs, lullabies and comfort and three meals a day, and comb her hair as gently as I possibly can. That's not enough, is it? It can't possibly be enough.

"Why isn't that enough?" my mother asks, at my kitchen table. She's very old, with a wobbly voice. Her wispy hair is completely white.

"Because she's so unhappy."

"Who wouldn't be, under the circumstances? She has every reason to be unhappy. Why do you put such a premium on happiness?"

"Because she's only eight years old, and she needs me."

The kettle whistles. I fill the teapot.

"Well, of course she does. But let the girl be sad, or mad, or whatever she needs to be. This takes time. You can't do a quick fix, or make it go away. And you can't make it perfect."

"Yes, you keep saying that."

"Is there anything I can do for my little granddaughter? Or for—"

"I know you want to help, but I told you—"

"I can make chicken soup."

"Eliana is a vegetarian."

"How 'bout for you?"

"Mom."

"You don't have to do this alone, Sweet—"

"Please go away."

She slowly fades away till there's just her outline on the chair, like a stencil shape filled in with fog, and then she's not there at all. The temperature drops. The tea is stone cold. I shiver. Suddenly, there's a steamy hot bowl of chicken soup in front of me, with a sprig of dill floating on top. It's delicious. I'm warm again.

"Wait. Please come back, Mom. I do want your help."

She's at the table again, in her nightgown, barefoot. I sit beside her and take both her hands in mine. Her wrinkled skin sags loosely from the bone, but her grip is strong. Her eyes are cloudy. She's in her late eighties, the age she would be today. We whisper, so as not to wake Eliana, asleep in the next room.

"Eliana is depressed, and I don't know how to help her."

"Yes, you do, Alice. You have the unenviable advantage of first-hand experience."

"Nothing like what Eliana is going through."

"Think back. Do you remember your senior year of college?

"I'd rather not."

"You got through it."

"That was totally different."

"Different. Not totally."

It was my senior year of college, and everything was falling apart. I lived in a tiny dorm room, due to a housing snafu; my parents' marriage seemed to be failing; my boyfriend Richard didn't pick up his phone; and was I imagining it, or were my friends acting weird around me?

Early one morning, I let myself into Richard's dorm room. It smelled of cigarettes, sweat, and semen. He and a girl were asleep, naked, a rumpled sheet half-covering them. They woke. The girl turned toward me. It was my friend, Maria. Nobody said anything. I felt sick. I walked out. It was raining.

I ran through the rain to the arts building on the other side of campus, drenched by the time I got there. One of my larger-than-life chair paintings from junior year was missing from the student gallery, and my environmental sculpture—made from two-by-fours, rope, marsh reeds, and a wooden chair—on display for the summer, was wrecked. The discarded ropes, boards and reeds lay in a heap. This was a nightmare. Did someone vandalize it, or did it just fall apart? Did my sculpture dismantle itself to teach me a lesson? What was the lesson? That I couldn't build anything to last? If that was the lesson, I'd quit. Since all my artwork disappeared or fell apart, I should switch to an art form that's meant to be ephemeral. Or was the lesson that I couldn't complete anything? That I was like my mother, who could never finish her P-H-Phucking D? That was a terrifying thought. I couldn't graduate from Princeton until I turned in a book-length senior thesis.

I was miserable. I wanted to leave school.

That night, I was lying in bed, in my crappy dorm room, when the phone rang. It was Tim, one of my housemates from this summer on Martha's Vineyard, calling from Brown. He was having a rough time, too, so he'd decided to take a semester off from school to travel around Peru. He asked if I wanted to join him.

I called home and asked for permission to take a semester off to go to Peru with Tim. They hesitantly agreed, as long as Princeton would refund my tuition.

Mom stayed on the phone after Dad said good-bye. I was defensive, expecting her to rail about what a scumbag Richard was for cheating on me. I braced myself, prepared to shut down and stop listening to her. I was accustomed to Mom despising my boyfriends for flaws real and imagined. Now that she was pissed off at my dad about some real or imagined transgression, and immersed in her angry feminist, anti-man "Don't get married until you have babies, and who wants babies" mode, she'd be even more likely to release her vitriol on my latest bad boyfriend.

Instead, she simply listened.

My mother listening and not talking? Lord Almighty, my mother was listening! This was unprecedented. She wasn't raging. She let me cry. Let me be sad. Let me call Richard a scumbag, without trying to beat me to it. I could hardly believe that she was so understanding. I had no idea she was such a good listener. She called me Sweetiepie, Honeylamb, Darling—terms of endearment I hadn't heard for years, which ignited a small flame of joy in me.

"Thank you, Mom. Thank you."

But I missed the deadline for a tuition refund by one day.

"This is totally screwed up!" I shouted, which didn't exactly endear me to the registrar.

I called home in tears.

"I'm so sorry," said Mom. Again, she listened. She let me cry. I wanted to confide my feelings to her, which I hadn't wanted to do for years.

"Why don't we get together?" she offered. "Would you meet me in the City tomorrow?"

I took the train from Princeton and met her at the Museum of Modern Art. I needed to get off campus. I'd been feeling horrible. I forced a smile when I saw her outside the museum. When she put her arms around me, I closed my eyes and crumpled against her chest. It was a warm, breezy September day. We sat outside in the museum's sculpture garden and sketched the sculptures: Maillol's voluptuous, larger-than-life nude bather, dipping her hair in the reflecting pool; Matisse's *Backs,* four monumental bas-relief sculptures of a female figure, the surface of her body like a craggy mountain, getting progressively more abstract and geometric in each iteration.

I asked Mom to pose for me. She sat on the edge of the fountain, tightened the scarf over her hair, and held down her wraparound skirt, which kept flapping open. She turned her face toward the bronze bather, while I drew her.

I hadn't really looked at her, not for a very long time, not closely like this. She looked different. I observed a softening in her face that I hadn't noticed when I was home in August. I drew her eyes; her large, warm, brown eyes. I sketched her jaw, more relaxed than I'd remembered, and her curly hair, grayer now. Did she look softer because she was getting older and her flesh was more flaccid, the skin more wrinkled? Yes, but there was also a gentleness that hadn't been there before. Her feelings for me had softened.

"I love your drawings. They're beautiful," she said.

Again, that small flame of joy. Then I remembered that I wasn't a visual artist any longer. I told her that I quit last week, because all my artwork falls to pieces. "If I'm going to be an artist at all, I'll make performance art that only lasts for the duration of the performance."

"Whatever you want," she said, wistfully. I would miss having Mom praise my drawings. The museum was closing. I hugged her, holding back tears. I didn't want to say good-bye.

The sun was going down when I got on the train back to Princeton, back to my crappy room, to my ruined artwork, to the humiliation of Richard and Maria's affair, to Tim's postcards from Peru, to the train wreck of my senior year.

I was so unhappy at Princeton that I went to the student counseling office. They referred me to a Jungian psychologist in town named Dr. Winterbottom, a ridiculous name for a shrink. I bicycled to her office and told her my dreams. Dr. Winterbottom explained that there was a war going on between my anima and animus. I thought this therapy might be bullshit.

The dour thesis adviser listened to my unorthodox senior thesis proposal—a theater piece exploring the commonalities between the rituals of animal behavior and human social rituals. My confidence waned as her scowl waxed.

"You need a new epistemology," she said dismissively.

I couldn't respond, because I had no idea what "epistemology" meant.

"The anthropology department expects your senior thesis to be a book-length dissertation."

I knew what a dissertation was. It was something you worked on your whole life and never finished. It was the family curse.

When I looked up *epistemology* that night, I was even more confused: "the theory of knowledge, esp. with regard to its methods, validity, and scope. The investigation of what distinguishes justified belief from opinion." How the fuck would I get a new one of those?

Mom laughed when I told her on the phone about my thesis advisor.

"What's so funny?"

"Academics can be such jerks. She's threatened by your creativity."

"Maybe so, but I'll need to come up with a new thesis topic."

"First, you have to find a new thesis advisor."

"Really?"

"I think so. Find an advisor who's more attuned to your interdisciplinary approach."

This was new: Mom giving me good advice. And me trusting her. She seemed to intuit just how I felt and how to make me feel better. I hadn't felt this way about my mother since I was a little kid. I could tell she enjoyed helping me.

I switched advisors and decided to write an academic thesis on theater and ritual—using the renowned anthropologist Victor Turner's theory of ritual to analyze contemporary experimental theater as ritual of social change. My new advisor, Ellen Basso, was able to introduce me to Turner, her mentor. He was so enthusiastic about my ideas that he invited me to apply to the interdisciplinary PhD program he headed up: the University of Chicago's Committee on Social Thought.

"That's marvelous! I'm so proud of you," said Mom. I glowed.

I DECIDED TO go winter camping over Christmas break—two weeks in the Adirondacks, where it was currently twenty degrees below zero. Some grad student had organized the trip and put up a flier. I'd signed up out of desperation. My depression hadn't improved in three months. It was worse. Nothing had helped: therapy, art, books, classes, food (which I'd been eating too much of, trying to numb myself). I had a hunch that a survival trip might break the curse. I wanted it to scare me out of my depression. It worked with hiccups.

We drove upstate in three cars loaded with backpacks, tents, sleeping bags, army-surplus leather snowshoes, warm clothes, cooking pots, stoves, canisters of kerosene, matches in Ziploc bags, peanut butter, chocolate bars, and instant ramen noodles. We hoisted our sixty-pound backpacks and hit the trailhead in a snowstorm. Soon, we all looked like snowmen, covered with fat white flakes.

For fourteen starlit nights, we stayed warm by square dancing in snowshoes around the campfire. By day, we hiked in snowshoes, stripped down to our T-shirts and sweating, even as our breath formed white clouds. One day, I saved a fellow camper from frostbite by thawing his foot on my warm stomach; that night he and I shared a tent, and it felt like it might be the start of something.

After fourteen sub-zero nights, after the excellent camaraderie that comes from living together in the wild, lining up our sleeping bags as close as possible to share body warmth—my depression was lifting. Life in the snow reformulated the equation, shifting the calculation toward optimism.

I rang in the New Year, 1976, at home with Mom, Dad, Madeline, and Jennifer, feeling better than I had all fall.

MAY ARRIVED, AND my mom proposed a visit. "This is very last-minute, and you're probably busy with your senior thesis. But I have the day free, and—"

"Yes, Mom, come visit! I turned in my thesis yesterday, so I'm not busy. And the weather is gorgeous."

I met her at the Princeton train station. She stepped off the train, carrying a picnic basket. She was wearing a paisley kerchief, denim wraparound skirt, and a button-down pale blue shirt. I was wearing an embroidered peasant blouse and jeans. It was two weeks before my graduation.

We sat in the grass and shared Brie cheese, French bread, and ratatouille. Our conversation was awkward. We were cautious with each other, unsure whether or not we were friends. Over the years, we'd become habituated to the glacial chill between us. It was different now. It was warming up. The beginning of something new. We were reinventing the mother–daughter rules, building a foundation for the years ahead.

"Did you hear from the University of Chicago?"

"I got in!"

"Congratulations! What did you say?"

"I said I was honored by the invitation, but I turned it down. I don't want to go into academia, Mom. I want to make theater. I'm starting a theater company with some other Princeton students."

She sighed, tilted her head, and looked at me with her thoughtful brown eyes. "Just as well. You won't risk spending your life trying to finish your PhD dissertation, like I did. Which reminds me, I'm about to start a new job—a full-time faculty position at a brand-new college. It's exciting to be there at the start of something new."

"Congrats, Mom, that's fantastic!"

We stashed the picnic basket in my dorm room and strolled around the campus. It was an awesome spring day after several rainy weeks. Everybody was outside, sunbathing, reading, and playing Frisbee. I had my camera with me, and I snapped pictures of campus, which was starting to look good to me again. I was graduating soon. I wanted to remember all this.

"Hey, Mom, I don't have any photos of the two of us together." I handed my camera to a classmate who was passing by. "Would you mind taking our picture?" We posed in front of the formal garden and smiled for the camera, with our arms around each other.

"Do you want to spend the night, Mom?"

We stayed up late, talking in the dark. It didn't matter what we talked about. The essential thing was that we were talking. Mom on the bed, me in a sleeping bag on the floor; telling stories, confiding in one another. *I wondered how we ever lost each other for all those years. And how did we find each other again on this balmy night in May, at the end of my senior year of college?* Our words and laughter filled the void, replenished the empty well, cool water bubbling up from deep below, splashing over the dry slate walls and filling us up, filling us up, filling us up.

It had been a long winter for Mom and me. Nine years. The ice was thawing. It was spring. It was finally spring.

I lost the roll of film I shot during that visit. Three years later, I found it under a radiator in my apartment. The photo lab was only able to salvage one picture. The color is radically distorted, as if the chemicals were intentionally manipulated during the developing. Mom and I are in the center of the photo, smiling, our arms around each other, she in her paisley kerchief and pale blue shirt; me in that peasant blouse. Framing us is a psychedelic blaze of bright red, orange, and purple streaks, as if we're being engulfed by flames.

FOUR

It's the New Year, 2009, and Eliana doesn't want to go back to school. I encourage her to talk about her feelings. She hates being different, doesn't want to be stared at because she needs a walker. She doesn't want to rejoin the class when she's so far behind. She's been isolated for six weeks, while the life of the classroom has gone on without her, and she feels estranged.

"I'm so sorry, Honey. It'll take a long time to get better. But you can talk to me as much as you want."

"I don't want to go to school. Please don't make me go."

I let her cry. I hold her. But she has to go back. She is assigned a full-time health paraprofessional to take her up and down the elevator (which makes her feel even more self-conscious), while the other fourth graders sprint boisterously up the stairs to their third-floor classroom.

The winter storms begin. I'm petrified that Eliana will fall and rebreak her surgically broken leg. There's a snowdrift in front of the school, right outside the cab door, and ice on the ramp to the handicap entry. How do I help her walk safely through a snowdrift with a walker? The wheels get clogged with the gunk in the dirty snow. The wheelchair-accessible door is jammed, and I have to throw my full weight into it to get it open. Why doesn't the school take care of the handicap entrance? I'm an irate parent, and I'm going to have a word with the principal.

"I hate myself for subjecting her to this," I confess to Michael.

Michael is torn between rolling his eyes in exasperation and wanting to comfort me. I'm grateful that he chooses the latter.

"We did what's best for Eliana in the long run," he says, wrapping his arms around me.

"She used to play soccer. Now she can't walk."

"She'll play soccer again," says Michael. "This is temporary."

"I hate myself."

"Let it go."

• • •

"ELIANA, THERE'S A counselor at school who can help you talk about your feelings if you want—"

"I don't need help talking! I have too much therapy already. Physical therapy at school *and* at home. I don't have time for more therapy." I can't argue with that. "Anyway, I only want to talk to you and Daddy about my feelings."

"You can talk to us about anything, any time you want."

"I know that."

ON THE X rays every other week at the surgeon's office, there's a widening gap between the upper and lower halves of Eliana's femur.

"This looks great. Perfect. Your bone is growing beautifully, Eliana," says Dr. Campbell.

Michael and I look at the same X ray, but all we see is a scary gap in the middle of her severed femur. *The Emperor's New Clothes* comes to mind.

"I don't see new bone," says Michael. "It looks like nothing's there."

"It's there," says Dr. Campbell. "You have to know how to look for it. The new bone is still soft, like cartilage, which is good. We don't want it to harden too quickly while we're still lengthening it. If that happens, and it sometimes does, we can't lengthen the leg any more."

That would be a total bummer.

After a few weeks of lengthening, her leg is visibly longer. I don't have time to go downtown to have Herman adjust her lift, so I bring her shoe to the Ecuadorian shoemaker on our block and ask him to reduce her shoe lift by half an inch.

"You want I make her lift smaller?" he asks, incredulously. "Explain, please," he says, handing me a pen and a newly cut leather shoe sole to draw on. I sketch a picture on the leather of Eliana's leg with the fixator attached; and another sketch of her bone with the gap in it, narrating as I draw.

He nods thoughtfully. "My niece in Ecuador, she has one arm shorter," he says. "Maybe one day she will have her arm lengthened."

THE FRESH-FALLEN SNOW is off limits to Eliana. Elevator doors are treacherous. Stairs are out of the question. Madeline tailors sweatpants for her, with extra fabric in the right leg to fit over the bulky fixator. She can't go outside for recess where the other kids are throwing snowballs. She has to sit in the cafeteria with the "home-work club" kids, who haven't finished their schoolwork.

Sometimes her friend Jojo gives up her outdoor recess to sit with Eliana in the cafeteria and keep her company. They're allowed to play quiet games together.

"I don't want to go to school," she says. Every day, I have to talk her into it. There are so many things she's not allowed to do, so I say yes to every reasonable request.

"Can I invite my friends over after school?"

"Yes, Sweetheart, of course you can."

Jojo comes over. They can't roughhouse like they used to, so they play dress-up. James and Eliana play board games and watch Harry Potter movies. When Galia comes over, I film their fancy costumed tea party. Eliana's Flip video camera is a big hit. Annika films Eliana expertly licking her right elbow. On her next visit, they ask me to film a contest: Without using their hands, Eliana and Annika have a race to see who can devour an ice-cream sundae fastest. I try not to laugh while I'm filming, but they're so funny, like voracious kittens, their faces in the bowls, slurping vanilla ice cream with their noses dipped in chocolate. It's a tie.

THE NEW BONE is finally visible on the X rays as a pale shadow, morphing from soft cartilage to solid bone. Eliana has finished the seven weeks of lengthening. No more quarter turns. But she still has six months of rehab ahead of her. There are endless physical therapy sessions and nightly pin care. Her daily regime has gotten more complex: in addition to an hour of stretching and strengthening exercises, she now has to wear an adjustable leg brace to straighten her knee for an hour, and another leg brace to *bend* her knee for a subsequent hour. For twenty minutes a day, she straps an ultrasound device onto her thigh, to escalate the rate of bone growth. (The insurance company tells us that the laptop-sized ultrasound machine is worth $20,000; we're careful not to drop it.) She does her homework while lying on the couch, attached to one or more contraptions. Every waking minute of her day is scheduled. She's sick of it, still sad and mad, but I think she's beginning to feel better. Physically. At least I hope she is. I'm ready for Eliana to feel better. This is a long winter.

"HELLO, I'M CALLING from school about Eliana."

"What's wrong?" I ask, in that instant, chest-tightening moment of panic every parent gets when they get a call from their child's school. It's a freezing January afternoon.

"Eliana is fine, but we have a little problem. Can Eliana walk down two flights of stairs?"

"No. Why?"

"The elevator is broken. But we have a plan. The fire department will carry her out of the building through the third-floor window."

I picture Eliana floating through the icy winter sky, hoisted by a fireman out of the third-floor window and onto a telescoping ladder, which slowly, slowly, slowly descends down to the fire truck. I imagine Eliana—who is scared of heights, and who wishes she could be inconspicuous and invisible—being transported out the window in the middle of the school day, attracting stares from children who watch with amazement out their classroom windows, shouting, "Look at Eliana!"

"Don't call the fire department. I'll take her down the stairs myself."

"Thank you, Ms. Cohen. We appreciate it."

I hang up and burst into tears. I have no idea how I'll get Eliana down the stairs. Mothers all over the world carry their children to safety, but I'm not strong enough to carry her down two flights. Michael is out of town. Maybe I should just let the fire department carry her out the window. I'm afraid that if I try to help her, she'll fall and break her compromised right femur, which appears, on the X ray, to be held in place purely by imagination.

My friend Eric offers to help. We meet the assistant principal in the school office. She has a different idea. "We think it's safest to carry Eliana down the stairs in a wheelchair."

Eric and I think that sounds riskier.

Eliana has another idea. "The easiest way is to slide down on my butt."

With no help from us, she slides down two flights of stairs, using the banister to pull herself arm over arm, like a monkey.

"That was the most fun I've had since before my operation!" she says, face flushed, green eyes shining.

"You were amazing!"

I tell her about the fireman's ladder idea, hoping to make her laugh, and expecting to score points with her for finding a less scary and conspicuous solution than being carried out a window.

"Aw, Mom! Why'd ya say no? It would have been so cool to go out the third-story window on a fireman's ladder!"

Damn! I should have let her do it. She's outgrown coddling. My protective instincts have segued to overprotective. I try to do the right thing, but the maternal perfection business is beyond me. Flying out the third-story window on a fireman's ladder through the frozen air might have scared her out of depression, like the hiccups, like my extreme winter camping trip did for me.

But, you know? Sliding down three flights of stairs like a monkey had the requisite touch of danger. It was good enough. I'm acclimating to the sufficiency of imperfection, settling for being adequate, which is not so bad, in the scheme of things. My mother taught me that. She's still teaching me that.

ELIANA IS NO longer in physical pain. Her spirits are rising. She has planned a Valentine's Day party. I make the cookie dough, while she writes the schedule and posts it on the wall:

Eliana's Valentine's Party!!!
Run around and scream—2 minutes
Make Valentine's cookies
Make Valentine's cards (while cookies are baking)
Pin the arrow on the heart
Eat cookies and cupcakes
Charades
If time, make up love stories

FIVE

I miss Julia. We all do. Spring break is next week and I can't wait. She's so busy with rowing practice that we rarely see her.

"Hi, Mom." It's the first time Julia has called home in a month.

"Hi, Honey. We're so excited to see you."

"Actually, I'm calling to tell you that Zoe invited me to meet her. She asked me to visit with her and her family in Florida for four days. I wanted to give you a head's up that I'll only be home for the last two days of break."

"Wow."

I'm thrilled for Julia and Zoe. And terribly disappointed for us. I feel usurped and insecure and excited and curious and confused and filled with love. I'm all these things at once.

"Not only will I meet my birth mother, I'll get to meet my two half-sisters. I'm so excited!"

What if Julia likes her biological family more than ours? They probably don't brood. Maybe Julia won't need us anymore. I feel obsolete and lonely, as if Julia has already chosen Zoe over me.

I picture Zoe at twenty, the age she was when we met her at the adoption agency, nineteen years ago. She was seven months pregnant. Brad and I had waited two years for a baby and had almost given up hope, when Zoe asked to meet us. We just needed her approval.

"I was adopted, when I was a baby," Zoe told us, at that first meeting. "I want the adoptive parents to be at the birth, so they can bond with this baby right away. Alice and Brad, I want both of you to be there." Zoe grinned at us and giggled. "I approve!"

I'M ON MY way out the door when Julia gets home. After five days in the Florida sun, her skin is golden, and her hair is streaked with blond. She's wearing flip-flops, tank top and shorts, which show off her newly athletic body. From all the rowing, she's become powerfully muscular. She looks glorious.

I give her an enormous hug. "I'm racing to pick up Eliana."

"I'll come with you."

"Great! She'll be thrilled."

We walk the six blocks, passing street vendors, nannies with strollers, a violinist playing Tchaikovsky, business men and women, a woman collecting bottles from garbage cans, a postal worker, New Yorkers of all stripes racing, biking, scootering, wheelchairing, window-shopping, sauntering, and jogging up and down Broadway.

"I had an amazing time," says Julia, as we walk.

"What was it like when you first saw each other?" I ask. "What is Zoe like? I want to hear everything. Was it wonderful, confusing, overwhelming, intense, joyful, all of the above? Did you have feelings you never had before?"

"Not until right now," she says, her eyes welling up. "When I was there, it was so familiar and easy. Zoe is a lot like me, temperamentally. I felt comfortable with her instantly. Actually, Zoe had to have a minor operation last week. I think it's called an "umbilical hernia." They had to put some stitches in, because her bellybutton keeps opening up—something like that. She kept apologizing because she was laid low, and I ended up taking care of the little girls a lot of the time, but they're adorable, and it made it more comfortable for me, because I knew what my role was."

"I thought about you all week, but I didn't want to intrude."

"I appreciate that a lot, Mom."

"Do you think Zoe would want me to call her?"

"Yes."

"You sure?"

"Definitely. She told me she hoped you'd call."

"I REMEMBER THE first time we met, when I said, '*I approve*,' and you guys looked so happy," Zoe said to me on the phone the next morning. "I love the photo and the letter you sent me when Julia was six months. I took them out every year on August twenty-third, and wished Julia a happy birthday."

"I've often wondered, Zoe, did you ever have regrets about the adoption?"

"Nope."

A moment of silent disbelief. "Never?"

"Never. I knew you'd be good parents."

This is oddly disturbing to me. I'd always assumed that Zoe had gone through a maelstrom of doubt—the kind of Sturm und Drang I would have felt in her situation. No qualms about giving her baby up for adoption? That's crazy! It's such a foreign concept to me. I have regrets about *everything!* I bought a small coffee this morning, and now I regret not getting a large. How could Zoe not have had second thoughts about giving up her newborn baby? I guess it's because she's not the Sturm und Drang type, but still.

"I remember the moment I knew you'd be a good mother. When I was in labor, and I barfed on you," Zoe giggled. "Do you remember?"

"I do."

"And it didn't bother you at all. You just cleaned me up and took care of me, in this very maternal way."

"That's how you knew I'd be a good mother?

"Yes."

"And that's why you never doubted your decision?"

"Yes, I just knew."

"Did you change your mind about us when you heard that Brad and I divorced?"

"Not at all. I felt bad for you guys, but I knew you'd both continue to take care of Julia. Look how beautifully she's grown up. You did a great job as parents."

"Thanks. Yeah, we did okay. Zoe, did you ever find your own birth mother?"

"Nope. I've never been interested in meeting her."

"Never?"

"Nope. Not interested."

"Really? I would have thought . . ."

My sentence trails off. I guess it's a blessing to have no ambivalence. But I can't help assigning symbolic value to Zoe's umbilical hernia. She was separated from her biological mother at birth. Twenty years later, she gave her first-born baby to us. At age thirty-nine, Zoe's bellybutton—where the umbilical cord once connected her to her birth mother—has not fully closed. That first wound won't heal.

"Zoe, I hope it's okay with you that I called today."

"Are you kidding? I was hoping you'd call. I'm thrilled to hear from you." She paused, then said, "I thought you might not approve."

"Approve of what?"

"Of Julia coming to see me."

Do I approve? I had always expected Julia to meet Zoe. I'd anticipated that it would be a rite of passage for Julia. I didn't expect it to be such a challenging rite of passage for me. It requires letting go—not my strong suit. Is this the garden-variety heartbreak every mother feels when her child leaves home? Or am I losing something more, as Julia, on the cusp of adulthood, begins this new relationship, rationing her limited free time between

Mom on the East Coast, Dad on the West Coast, and Birth Mother in Florida? Or am I brooding simply because I have an innate need to brood?

"Mom, how long have I had the fixator?" Eliana has recently graduated from a walker to crutches.
"Five months."
"When does it come off?"
"May. Next month."

It's May. The fixator and the six bolts have finally been removed from her leg! Eliana now wears a hot-pink full-leg plaster cast. The femur will be compromised and fragile for another few months while new bone fills in the holes. She's in the cast for ten days. After that, she'll have to relearn how to walk.

Thousands of migrating birds are passing through Central Park, communing in this avian oasis, singing like crazy. Through the trees are flashes of bright yellow, orange, red, blue feathers. The park ranger tells me that the eccentric wild turkey has finally flown away—probably in search of a mate. Hooray turkey!

SIX

"I'm treating you to lunch, Mom."

"Thank you, Sweetheart. No argument from me."

I was twenty-two years old. It was June 1977. We were at my favorite Indian restaurant, in Greenwich Village. Mom and I had finally made peace with each other. Ever since she visited me at Princeton a year ago and spent the night in my dorm room, something had clicked. There'd been a sea change. She and Dad seemed also to have made peace with each other. She had made peace with herself.

I'd graduated Princeton the previous June, and my first year out of school was wonderful. I was living in a loft in New York City. For the first time in my life, I was supporting myself—barely, but still.

The turbaned sitar player and tabla player sat cross-legged on the Persian rug covering the wide window seat.

My mother and I sat at a table near the duo, enthralled by the music and by the plates of food passing by: steamy curries, sizzling tandoori platters, deep-fried pakoras, and puffy golden poori bread, each one more aromatic than the next.

"Mmmm, everything looks and smells so delicious," said Mom. She looked older and grayer, but more re-laxed, wearing a loose-fitting, Indian-print cotton dress and a long necklace of carved wooden beads.

The waiter brought our menus.

"The lunch special is enough for two to share, if that's okay with you, Mom—"

"Whatever you order is fine with me."

"Sir? We'll have the vegetable pakoras, shaag paneer, lamb curry, poori, and two mango lassis." The waiter left with our order.

"How's the loft working out?"

"It's a fantastic rehearsal space. I hope you and Dad can come see the new piece I'm working on with Anne."

"I'm sure we can."

"Anne is an incredible dancer and choreographer. She has this beautiful combination of stillness and intensity. I love collaborating with her."

"Does she live in the loft?

"Nope, no room. At last count, I have eight roommates."

"Eight!"

"It's become a crash pad for the downtown dance and theater crowd."

"Is it worth the hassle?"

"Well, it's cheap. I only have to type two days a week."

"How's the job?

"It's a typing job, with incidental teaching. I love the teaching and I have plenty of time to rehearse, so all in all, it's pretty good. Yum, aren't the pakoras terrific?"

"Delicious."

"We each pay only fifty dollars a month, but forget about privacy. And then there's the brothel downstairs—"

"Brothel?"

"Oops, forgot to mention—"

"Alice!"

"That's why the rent's so cheap."

"Don't you think it's time to move?"

"Actually, Seth and I are looking for an apartment together."

"Mazel tov! I'm happy for you."

"You mean that?"

"Of course. Why wouldn't I mean it? I like Seth."

"You do?"

"Sure. He's a nice guy, and you're clearly fond of each other. What's not to like?"

"Wow. This is the first time you've approved of any of my boyfriends."

"Huh. I suppose you're right. You've grown up. I have, too. As long as he makes you happy, I'm happy for you."

"Thanks, Mom, that means the world to me. What about you? How's your new job?"

"Best job I've ever had."

"Really?"

"Yeah. I love everything about Empire State College. I love mentoring. I love my students and my colleagues. It's my dream job. They even pay me well, how d'ya like that—a first for me, after all those adjunct positions. I'm so grateful this job doesn't require a doctorate. You know how long I worked on that damn dissertation."

"Yup."

"I've finally found myself, at age fifty-seven. Call me a late bloomer."

"You're a late bloomer!"

"This is the first time in years that I am truly happy."

"Do you mean that?"

"I was depressed for such a long time—even before I had cancer."

"I didn't know."

"Oh, c'mon, Alice. I'm sure you knew, on some level. I'm convinced that my depression caused my cancer. Which reminds me—Great news! I just got a clean bill of health. Cancer-free for ten years!"

"Wonderful!"

"After the cancer, I was terribly unhappy. I was so disfigured, I no longer felt like a woman. But now—please indulge me, Alice, I want to tell you a story—I have a colleague at work named Seymour. His office is next to mine, and he flirts with me. Look at me, I'm blushing. It's not an affair, but it's a genuine flirtation. It makes me happy. Flirting with Seymour makes me feel alive. I feel more alive than I've felt in a very long time."

After hugging Mom good-bye, I walked up Second Avenue toward the loft, feeling so buoyant it was all I could do to keep from skipping—or floating—and I realized how remarkable that lunch was. After a decade of Sturm und Drang, we loved each other again. It was official! This wasn't just a truce. We were no longer warily testing the waters. It had been a whole year that we enjoyed being together. As awful as our adolescent relationship had been, from this day onward, it was going to be great. And I was so thrilled for Mom. She was finally happy. God, this was a new dawn for her. She survived cancer. No recurrence for ten years—hooray! She finally achieved the professional success that eluded her all these years. After going through hell, she was at the height of her powers. Her happiness made me happy.

TWO WEEKS LATER, my mother died, suddenly and unexpectedly, in the early morning. Dad said they were both asleep, when she bolted upright with her head in her hands, groaned in pain, and fell back on her pillow. She never regained consciousness. A fault on her main artery burst. She died of cerebral hemorrhaging from a ruptured aneurism.

AND THEN I was in Colorado, two months after her death, trying to create a piece about her. My choreographer friend Anne and I were living for one month in Boulder, in an old miner's cabin high up a mountain, two vertical miles out of the city. We pumped water from a well and bathed outdoors under a canvas army-surplus shower. We drove down the mountain every day to rehearse in a sun-drenched, maple-floored dance studio in town. We were creating a dance-theater piece called *Separation in Four Parts*.

I had never lived in such a beautiful place as this. And

I'd never felt so lost and unrooted, as if I might float away. I scrambled up to the summit behind the cabin and watched an eagle circling over the ravine. I sat at the edge of the cliff, fighting vertigo, fighting the urge to leap off the edge and fly. I wondered what it must be like to soar on air currents like the eagle, defying gravity, unafraid. The eagle made me think about Mom.

It's risky business, transforming grief into something else before its time, giving it a shape, putting it outside yourself, to examine and edit and craft into something beautiful, performing it for an audience before you've finished grieving. It's an occupational hazard of being an artist.

Being in Boulder and creating this performance was a wonderful way to honor my mother, but it wasn't helping me to mourn. Some days, I felt strangely detached from her death, as if it didn't really happen. Death was the subject of our new show, but constructing the piece was helping me to keep her alive. I struggled with this.

"The Giant and Puppet Show" was Part 1 of *Separation in Four Parts*. Anne was a beautiful dancer, riveting to watch, even in a rehearsal room, even when she was perfectly still. Anne was the Giant. She sat silently on top of a tall ladder, wearing an embroidered Tibetan prayer robe with long sleeves that extended past her hands, and an enormously long black skirt that covered the ladder and draped onto the floor.

The skirt doubled as a puppet stage. I sat on the floor below the ladder with a hand puppet, which reached through the opening in the long skirt, searching for the Giant, trying to get her attention by telling jokes, singing love songs, throwing tantrums.

But the Giant was transcendent and unreachable. Arms extended like wings, her torso turned in the slowest possible slow motion, like a shape-shifting cloud, or an eagle weightlessly riding the wind.

I try to remember what my mother was like in that very brief time—the last year of her life, the year when she was happy for the first time in years. She and I were finally close again. She had just come back from her long sojourn in the land of illness and despair and anger—and so had I. I want to remember her the way she was then, in her brief, glimmering coda of true happiness.

I pull an old scrapbook off the bookshelf in the living room and open to a clipping from the Empire State College newspaper from 1977. There's a photo of Mom.

No longer beautiful, she's a pleasant-looking woman of fifty-seven, with warm eyes, wrinkly skin, short curly gray hair. She's looking slightly to the left, listening intently to someone off-camera, perhaps a student she's mentoring. The text surrounding the photo is the eulogy given at her funeral by her friend and colleague Lois Lamdin, an associate dean at the college. I remember trying to listen to her eulogy at the funeral, but I was crying too hard to hear. I had been asked if I wanted to say something, but I couldn't do it. If I spoke at her funeral, it would mean she was actually dead.

I curl up on the sofa and read.

"Those of us who worked with Louise Cohen carry in our hearts indelible images of this woman we loved so dearly. We remember Louise spending hour upon hour of patient, loving time with students, laughing and crying with them, opening up vistas of the intellectual world she inhabited. When problem students came along, we assigned them to Louise, and then, magically, they were no longer problem students. Louise said all her students were either beautiful or brilliant, but most often both. And with her loving encouragement and support, they usually became brilliant and beautiful.

"We will remember the Louise who brought us cookies

and the solace of her presence when we were down, and told us how beautiful and brilliant we were. And Louise at graduation, such a few weeks ago, smiling with embarrassment as student after student stopped at the microphone to pay special tribute to their mentor.

"We will remember Louise as a woman totally devoid of materialism. When others talked about new clothes and cars and houses, she talked about ideas and feelings and philosophical first principles. Her only pride was in her family, in Ira and Madeline and Alice and Jennifer.

"Louise never met a person she didn't like, and she could discern and draw out the best qualities in all of us. We remember her ingenuousness, her honesty, her sense of wonder that the world and all the people in it were good. And we will remember how, when any issue, any policy, any course of action was discussed, Louise would ask the basic question: 'Will any one be hurt by this?' And if the answer was yes, then arguments of mere logic or expediency could not move her. She became, gradually, this gentle woman, our conscience, the one voice that spoke up always, fearlessly and at any cost, from her impassioned sense of justice, for the rights of the individual human being."

I put the scrapbook away and climb into my bed, pulling the down comforter up to my chin. This was my mother. This loving and beloved woman was my mother, as were all her other shape-shifting incarnations. My brilliant, adoring mother, who protected her three babies with fierce dedication. The woman who visited the jaws of death and returned angry and cold, an unrecognizable ghost of herself. The loving mentor, filled with life and happiness and confidence, who—as soon as she returned fully to life—suddenly died.

I roll onto my stomach and cry silently, my face pressed into the pillow. *I miss you. I miss you. I miss you so much.*

SEVEN

I have an indelible image of my mother in her final hour, buried under life support equipment, eyes closed, her face expressionless.

But this is an image I never saw. The last time I ever saw my mother was at the Indian restaurant.

The day my mother died, Madeline and I went to the hospital. At the door to the ICU, we were greeted by a nurse.

"Girls," she said, gently, "You can go in to say good-bye to your mother if you want, but you won't recognize her. She's brain dead. She's gone. She's not your mother anymore. You don't want to remember her this way."

I took the nurse's advice and didn't go in. I had just seen her two weeks before, when she told me she felt happier and more alive than she had in years. That's how I wanted to remember her. Madeline went into the ICU to say good-bye, while I waited outside.

The day my mother died was the first time I ever saw my father cry. He held me and my sisters in his strong arms, protecting us as if we were still little girls. We, in turn, protected him. We clung to each other, our faces puffy, our eyes narrow slits from so much crying.

Later that day, when our crying had briefly subsided, Dad suggested that we begin to sort through Mom's things. I didn't question the timing of this; why, even before she was buried, we were combing through her closets and papers and jewelry box, deciding what to keep, what to discard, and what to give away. I trusted Dad. It seemed a sensible way to move forward.

We each went to a different room. From my mother's study, I could hear the alternating crescendo and decrescendo of Madeline's sniffling, Jennifer's sobbing, Dad's keening. I quietly pored over the mishmash in a tan leather purse: a memo book, three ballpoint pens, peppermint Life Savers, a shopping list, sunglasses, an old picture of my sisters and me on the beach in matching blue bathing suits—and an unsealed envelope, simply addressed, in my mother's handwriting, "Ira." I opened the envelope and unfolded her typed letter.

If you don't end your affair, I will end our marriage.

The words flew off the page and reassembled into the

angry voice of my mother, speaking to me—like the ghost of Hamlet's father, "List, list, O, list! If thou didst ever thy dear father love, revenge his foul and most unnatural murder!"

This wasn't *Hamlet.* Mom wasn't murdered. But she was wronged, and she was asking me to avenge her. *"If thou didst ever thy dear mother love . . ."*

I didn't know if the accusation was true, though I'd long suspected it; and if true, what I was supposed to do with it. I didn't know how old the letter was. But I read it today, of all terrible days, and I couldn't unread it.

What am I supposed to do? What do you want me to do?

I wished there'd been skull and crossbones on the envelope, warning of its poisonous contents. But I opened it and released her fury, which was now my burden, mine to interpret and act on. Unless I simply gave the letter to my father. It was addressed to him, it was *his* letter, not mine. I never should have read it. I would just give it to him.

But from the next room, I heard Dad burst into tears like a little boy, and my sisters comforting him, and I couldn't show the letter to him. It would be cruel. I tore it to pieces and threw it away, thinking that would be the end of it. But my mother's voice stayed inside me—like a *dybbuk,* a wandering spirit that enters and possesses the body of a living person.

At my mother's funeral, I had trouble believing she was dead. I forced myself to look at her casket, and to shovel dirt on her grave, so that I would remember burying her. But none of it seemed real. The next day, I couldn't remember the funeral, I couldn't picture the cemetery, couldn't remember shoveling any dirt, though I did remember the percussive sound of pebbles falling on wood. Instead, I heard her voice from the letter. And I pictured her in the ICU, where I never saw her.

I tried to stop hearing the angry voice of the letter. I tried to get her out of my head, but I couldn't. I was possessed.

I KEPT THE letter a secret for two years. In some desperate and inconsolable part of my mind, the secret kept her alive. I was in limbo, my grief in suspended animation, my life held hostage by magical thinking. I longed to retrieve my gentle, loving mother who was happy for the first time in years, and with whom I'd finally reconciled. But I only heard her bitter, angry voice, asking me to avenge her.

When I couldn't bear it any longer, I told my dad.

We sat in his kitchen, our coffee getting cold. Our old cat, Amanda, rubbed against my legs under the table and purred. My dad was sad for me.

"I wonder why Louise was still carrying it. That was probably an old purse. She gave me that letter years ago."

"You already read that letter?"

"Yeah. We worked it out."

"You already read it," I groaned. The secret I was protecting my father from wasn't even a secret. What a humiliating anticlimax. Amanda jumped in my lap and licked my face, like she always did when I cried.

"Gee, Alice, I wish you'd given me the envelope when you found it. What a terrible burden you carried for two years."

"Dad. Did you have an affair?"

"Yes."

I stared at the table for a moment, then looked up at him.

"I'm angry. And sad."

"Of course you are. I'm sorry this has caused you so much anguish."

"I need to tell my sisters."

"I understand."

It was a letter she wrote to my father, not my mother's

ghost commanding me to avenge her. But in that moment of unbearable grief—grief being just a hair's breadth away from madness—I wanted it to be my mother's voice talking to me. We had just begun to talk to each other again, and I didn't want it to end. I had lost her once, when I was twelve years old. I couldn't bear to lose her a second time.

I'D BEEN STALLED in the grieving process. I missed the moment to say good-bye to Mom the day she died. No do-over. There was just moving forward. I needed relief from those two years. I didn't want my mother's voice inside me anymore. I wanted to stop thinking about her. I could try to forget her. Gradually, I did.

EIGHT

"Everything's gone like clockwork, don't you agree?" says Dr. Campbell cheerfully to Eliana and me at her final post-op visit in May.

Eliana and I stare dumbly, trying to process his breezy assessment.

"So," he continues. "You can go to camp this summer. You have only three restrictions: avoid contact sports, no jumping from high places, and don't fall down."

"But what if I *do* fall down?"

"Don't. Just don't. That's all there is to it, no falling. Falling would be bad. The X ray looks great. You look great."

She does look great, sitting on the examining table in oversized, hospital-issue gym shorts, finally rid of all that hardware. And even I can see that the new X ray looks excellent. The once scary gap in her femur is filled in with solid bone, good as new and five centimeters longer.

"Looking ahead," he says to me, "you'll have to make a decision about the second surgery. The next one is at your discretion."

"Does 'at your discretion' mean the second surgery is optional?" I ask.

"No, of course not. We're not going to let Eliana wear a shoe lift her whole life. It's the *timing* of the second surgery that's up to you. As you know, I recommend completing the lengthening process before she enters high school. Come back in October for X rays. Have a good summer."

"Can you close the door, Mom?" Eliana whispers, as soon as Dr. Campbell leaves the room.

I close the door.

"Can anyone hear us?"

"No."

"Good." She sits very still on the examination table, her shoulders tense.

"What is it, Honey?"

"I will never, ever, have leg-lengthening surgery again."

"We don't have to talk about it now. We can think about it again in a year."

"I won't change my mind in a year. I mean it, Mom. I refuse to have this surgery ever again."

"I promise you won't have surgery during middle school. You don't have to think about it for four years. You might change your mind when you're in high school."

"Mom!" She looks me in the eye, silencing me, making sure she has my undivided attention. "I won't change my mind."

ELIANA IS NOT yet happy, but she's on the mend.

Julia is über-happy.

Michael is reasonably happy.

I allow myself cautious optimism. We made it through the darkest times of this terrible year. Maybe, just maybe, I'm, I'm—

ON THE LAST day of May, my alarm radio wakes me with the terrible news: *"Dr. George Tiller, the prominent and polarizing abortion provider, was killed Sunday, gunned down during morning services at his church in Wichita, Kansas . . ."*

No!

I think back to that terrifying time, ten years ago, when I found out that I was six months pregnant. I had every reason to believe the fetus was injured, could imagine no good outcome, feared I'd never be able to love my baby, felt so hopeless that I thought about killing myself. I scheduled an abortion with Dr. Tiller in Wichita, and I began to feel less trapped. The suicidal thoughts abated. I decided to have the baby.

If I hadn't been given a choice, would I have taken my life?

I don't know.

If I hadn't chosen to give birth, would I love Eliana as deeply and completely as I do now, or would my feelings have been subverted by despair, guilt, and anger?

I don't know.

I never met Dr. Tiller, but I believe he saved both of our lives. I need to tell Eliana about him. I want her to know he was part of her life. I'm not keeping secrets from her anymore.

"Eliana, do you know what an abortion is?"

"Duh, I'm in fourth grade."

"Well, when I was in fourth grade, I didn't even know— Oh, never mind. I want to talk to you about something important."

I tell her about Dr. Tiller, about his work and about his murder. I tell her the story of her birth. Everything: the good parts and the bad parts. No more secrets.

"Does it upset you to know that I wanted to have an abortion?"

"No, I was just a fetus. I don't care what you thought of me before I was born. I care what you think of me now."

I hold her close. "I love you so much."

"I know."

Before this moment, I've never forgiven myself for that time when I didn't want Eliana. When I didn't want to be her mother.

I think about the terrible years after Mom's surgery, when my loving mother disappeared and was replaced by a gray stranger who—it seemed to me—no longer wanted to be my mother. I finally understand that she was always there. That she couldn't help being sick and sad. That she was doing the best she could. That those years were as painful for her as they were for me.

I've never forgiven myself—or my mother—for the crime of maternal ambivalence.

I forgive my mother.

I forgive myself.

"I KNOW IT'S not logical."

"You're kidding, right?" asks Michael.

"No. Whenever I start to feel really happy, I'm scared that the Evil Eye will get me. Like the way my mom died, just two weeks after saying that she was happy for the first time in years."

"You're not joking?"

"I wish I were."

"I thought you used the Evil Eye as a literary device."

"That, too."

"I mean, if you enjoy thinking about the Evil Eye—"

"No! I don't enjoy it, not at all. It makes me feel stupid and cowardly."

I start to cry. Michael must think I'm a moron. He's probably stifling a laugh, but he pulls me onto his lap and hugs me.

"Listen up, Alice. Don't worry about the Evil Eye anymore. It's a waste of your time. Don't think about it. You'll be fine. Nothing bad will happen. Just don't worry."

"Okay, I won't."

"Good." And he kisses me. He kisses me again. He's a great kisser. I'm so in love with this guy. He pulls me down beside him and we kiss some more, and we unbutton, unzip, undress, caress, make love.

I lie with my head on his chest, content and happy.

I'm happy.

Lightning didn't strike. I didn't spit three times through

my middle and index finger. I didn't throw salt over my left shoulder. I didn't turn a glass upside down. Nothing bad happened.

Take that, Evil Eye!

MICHAEL AND I visit the girls at camp in Maine. Julia is a counselor, Eliana a camper. We watch Julia teach an organic baking class, and I sample the most delicious cookies I have ever tasted. We hike to the lake to watch Eliana's swim class.

"I have exciting news," Julia tells us at our picnic lunch. "Next week, I'm going to meet my biological grandmother."

"No way."

"Yes way. She lives in Maine, and she's driving to camp to meet me. She's my birth father's mother. Zoe has been in touch with her and told her I was working here."

"That's fantastic."

"I know! Isn't it?"

"You think you'll ever meet your birth father?"

"One day, probably."

"Wow!" This is all good, but my head is spinning.

"Oh, by the way, Mom," says Eliana, "there's something I need to tell you. I didn't think I should write this in a letter, because I thought it might make you nervous."

"I'm nervous already. What is it?"

"We went to an island and I jumped from a thirty-foot cliff into a lake."

"You jumped from a thirty-foot cliff?"

"Yup. Like about twenty times. It was so fun."

My heart ricochets around my chest like a pinball machine. "And . . . and your leg felt okay?"

"Totally! Oh, and last week I was trampled by a llama."

"Trampled by a llama?"

"Yeah, by Alex, my favorite llama."

"What part of you did Alex trample?"

"My right leg. I was taking him for a walk, and his feet sank in the mud, which freaked him out. He panicked, tried to run, knocked me down, and trampled my right leg. It hurt for a few minutes, but I'm totally fine now. I figured it would be better to tell you in person."

"You know me well."

After lunch, Julia enlists us to help paint the set for the camp play. She's codirecting, and Eliana is acting in it.

We paint cardboard cartons, under a dazzling blue sky.

"Gorgeous day," I say.

"It's gonna rain," says Julia, painting a box with efficient brush strokes.

"Yup, it'll definitely rain," says Eliana, getting as much paint on her jeans as on the box.

"You're kidding, right?" I say.

"Nope," says Julia.

"It'll rain," says Eliana.

"But there's not a cloud in sight," says Michael.

Crash of thunder.

"Grab the boxes!" shouts Julia.

It's a downpour. We run inside. Soaked. Laughing. Happy.

Let's see if I have this right: My daughters love the calm before the storm, and they love the storm, and the calm after the storm, which is a truer sort of calm. And because they no longer need me to protect them from changing and unpredictable forces of nature and emotion, and thirty-foot cliffs, and freaked-out llamas, I am free to let go of my habitual, anticipatory dread of both storm and calm.

NINE

I dream about my mother. She's a little girl in a white cotton dress, running with her Grandfather Jake in his peach orchard in Oklahoma. She's a teenager, studying late at night in her dark, unhappy house in Brooklyn. She's a fashionable Barnard student, typing papers. She goes on a date with Ira, the handsome Coast Guard officer back from the war, the one she was waiting for. She's on a research team with Margaret Mead. She gives birth to Madeline and is madly in love with her first-born child. She has a miscarriage, and then another, and another. She holds me in her arms, relieved that I made it. She comes home on a winter day with baby Jennifer. She takes me campaigning for civil rights. She plays tennis with Ira. She makes chicken soup. She naps on the hammock and birds alight on her book. She types and types and can't finish her dissertation. She gets sick. She's furious because

I suddenly have breasts and she suddenly has none. She suspects Ira of infidelity. She types and types. She visits me at college, we have a picnic, somebody takes our picture. I treat her to lunch at the Indian restaurant. She's happy for the first time in years. She is sleeping beside Ira, suddenly sits up with her head in her hands, slumps back on her pillow. She has had a ruptured aneurism. I see it through her eyes, I see the blood and her blurred vision, I feel the unbearable pressure in her head, I hear the sound of the ambulance siren and then nothing.

THE LAST TIME I saw my mother was the day I took her to the Indian restaurant, when she was fifty-seven and I was twenty-two, a year out of college, on the cusp of adulthood.

That was the year my mother came back.

She came back as herself, the way I remembered her, the way I wanted her to be, after years of sickness and sadness and anger; and after my years of stormy teenage sadness and anger. She finally came back. For one year. And at the end of that year, she died.

I WALK THROUGH the Ramble on a windy July morning, and sit on a wooden bench in a grove of trees.

The air smells like honeysuckle. A sparrow lands on the bench beside me. It hops closer. I remember when birds loved to land beside my mother on the hammock.

A wind rustles through the leaves, which flash their shimmering silver underbellies like they do before a storm. There's a stirring in the trees, with much birdsong and flying about. The sparrow flies away. I wipe tears from my eyes.

Mom, Mommy, Louise.

She flies under the leaves toward me, shimmering but invisible. The wind picks up, and I feel the warmth of her and the chill of her.

A warm, salty breeze wraps itself around me. It's my mother's hug. I want her here with me. It doesn't matter whether she's a ghost, or a memory, or my idea, or her idea, or God's idea, or dust, or sound waves, or transfigured molecules, or an echo from the Cosmos. She's here with me.

Mom throws salt over her left shoulder and over my left shoulder. In the next gust of wind, the salt floats and billows and swirls around me, blowing my long hair in all directions, and protecting me with salty swirls of luck and courage.

My mother is back.

"I love you," I whisper.

"I love you," echoes the wind.

at the New School Writing Program for their support and inspiration; to my students, from whom I'm constantly learning; to my friends Galia and Steve Moors, whose living room salons were safe havens for trying out early chapters-in-progress.

I'm indebted to the Writers Room, where I began this project, and to the Virginia Center for Creative Arts, for three weeks of uninterrupted writing in a utopic setting, with three meals a day, a room with a view, and the exhilarating company of fellow artists.

I'm grateful every day to my remarkable sisters, Madeline Cohen and Jennifer Cohen, my best friends and confidantes, who helped me remember details about our childhood and who offered thoughtful feedback and support throughout the project.

Boundless love and gratitude to my amazing family—my husband Michael and daughters Julia and Eliana—for allowing me to tell the story of our turbulent year. (Of course, if you ask them to tell the story, they would each tell it differently.) Eliana, thanks also for allowing me to publish your poem.

Deepest love and gratitude to my late parents: my affectionate, encouraging, and whimsical father, Ira Cohen; and my wonderful, complicated, loving mother, Louise Giventer Cohen.

ACKNOWLEDGMENTS

Thanks to my brilliant editor, Andra Miller, for her insight, wisdom, and enormous patience; and to Sally Wofford-Girand, my remarkable agent, for her expert advice and personal warmth, and for finding the perfect home for this book at Algonquin.

Many thanks to my smart friends who generously read drafts and shared invaluable insights and suggestions: Juliette Carrillo, Barbara Kancelbaum, Melissa Kraft, Kathy Mendeloff, Jacqueline Reingold, Ricki Rosen, Susan Stephen, and Heather Tait. To my writer friends and colleagues who brainstormed with me over cups of coffee and glasses of wine, and gave me courage when I most needed it, thanks to Libba Bray, Randi Epstein, Marie Myung-Ok Lee, Ruth Ozeki, and Jon Reiner. Thanks to the Upper West Side Writers Gang for our collective mulling, laughing, and cheering on; to Abigail Thomas for teaching me how to write courageously; to my colleagues